THE LOST WAYS

David Kennedy

Copyright © 2018 David Kennedy

All rights reserved.

ISBN: 9781983149962

CONTENTS

1	INTRODUCTION	1
2	PSYCHOLOGICAL PREPARATION & PLANNING	5
3	HUMAN HEALTH ESSENTIAL ELEMENTS	20
4	FIRST-AID FACILITATION	31
5	STEREOTYPED SURVIVAL SETTINGS & SITUATIONS	74
6	DETERMINING DANGEROUS DIMENSIONS	94
7	FIVE FUNDAMENTAL SURVIVAL SKILLS	110
8	SIGNIFICANT SURVIVAL SCIENCES	164
9	ADAPTIVE CAPACITY: A CONCLUSION	179

© **Copyright 2018 by David Kennedy**

All Rights Reserved

In accordance with the U.S. Copyright Act of 1976, the reproduction, scanning, photocopying, recording, storing in retrieval systems, copying, transmitting, or circulating in any form by any means— electronic, mechanical, or otherwise— any part of this publication without a written permission from the publisher, constitutes piracy or theft of the author's intellectual property rights.

Exceptions only include cases of brief quotations embodied in critical reviews and/or other certain non-commercial uses permitted by copyright law. Alternatively, when using any material from this book other than reviewing simply, obtain prior permission by contacting the author, **James Evans**.

Both author and publisher shall be, in no case, held liable for any fraud or fraudulent misrepresentations, monetary losses, damages, and liabilities— indirect, consequential, or special— arising from event/s beyond reasonable control, or relatively set out in this book.

If advice is necessary, consult a qualified professional for further questions concerning specific or critical matters on the subject.

Notarial Notes

David Kennedy

The contents presented herein constitute the rights of the First Amendment.

All information states to be truthful, accurate, reliable, and consistent. Any liability, by way of inattention or otherwise, to any use or abuse of any policies, processes, or directions contained within, is the sole responsibility of the recipient reader.

The presentation of the entire information herein is without a contract or any form of guarantees or assurances. Therefore, any information hereupon solely offers for informative purposes only, and as such, universal.

The trademarks used herein, are without any consent. Thus, the publication of the trademark is without any permission or backing by the trademark owner/s.

All trademarks and brands mentioned in this book are for clarification purposes only and owned by the owners themselves, not affiliated with the author or publisher.

Thank you for supporting the rights of the author and publisher.

INTRODUCTION

Life is sacred… life is precious. Why do we say this is so? It is simply because we are human beings!

Unlike animals, which only have the innate impulse to survive and procreate, humanity has the ability to attach meaning to life. We are able to reflect on how fortunate we are just by the thought of being alive.

We feel happy with mere existence itself. However, sheer existence is just not enough for all of us.

We continue living life and justify our existence by encountering all the various crises and challenges—natural, circumstantial, and manmade—befalling us. Truly, at some point in our lives, we experience the pains of existence.

Towards our daily journeys to the unknown, imminent dangers, if not, disasters lie ahead and can catch us unwittingly. Yet, we ask, are all these sufferings worth living?

The fact that we are all mortals, we sometimes feel desperate and pessimistic about life. Ultimately, we become fatalists. In reality, all of us have the choice to exist. We just ought to make the effort of preserving the sacredness and preciousness of life.

On one hand, religion and our beliefs promise something eventually greater, which makes our lives lighter and easier. On the other hand, the human spirit, venturing in search of the true meaning of life, always prescribes hope—an altering attitude with a strong will—to adopt and adapt in order to survive and thrive!

Nevertheless, you may wonder why some people who have obtained complete and proper survival training programs were never able to apply their skills and merely perished. Yet, others, with only a few to no survival training lessons, were able to cope and come through life-threatening circumstances.

While learning survival skills is significant, possessing the will to survive is essential. Fact is that it necessitates much more than acquiring the extensive skills and knowledge to set-up shelters, forage for food, source water, build a fire, and travel sans the aid of any standard navigational gadgets to thrive successfully through a survival setup.

It is neither your survival kit nor the magnitude of the peril, the type of surroundings you have found yourself in, nor the number of companions you are with that determines your survival whenever an emergency happens. Instead, your vital recipe for any survival scenario is preparation—your proper and prepared perceptions in responding to catastrophic situations.

This life-saving manual, '*Survive & Thrive: Hone Your Art of Prepping & Coming through Alive—Your Comprehensive Prepping Way of Life and Survival Skills Manual for Whatever Catastrophes Whenever & Wherever,*' comprehensively contains all the basic information you ever need to know about the art of survival.

Initially, you will be conscious of, and learn to recognize certain stresses usually associated with survival. Along the learning process, you will discover how to prepare yourself precisely for any survival settings you might face-off, anytime and anywhere around the world.

Your mental preparedness actually influences all the aspects of survival. Therefore, everything boils down to espousing a positive mental attitude (PMA), which is your key to survival. Essentially, it is a foundational personal skill that you must hone in developing your will to survive.

Your persistent purpose to exist becomes the driving force to distinguish the value of life from the imminence of death for both your person and anybody who only relies upon your capacities to handle and resolve the fix. For this reason, you render the scary and unpredictable worlds of disasters and the unknowns as mere instruments, which you can use in your favor.

Regardless of the seeming direness of a situation, your mental preparedness and attitude allow you to be aware of your surroundings, make use of available resources, and to work them all out to your own advantage. All prior psychological preparations you have done will ensure your sky-high chances of survival.

Certainly, you will know how to perform the established survival procedures and techniques, as well as exercising strategic analytical skills, to convert a hellish existence into a heavenly haven. These life-preserving lessons will keep you safe, sound, and sane until either you are able to receive assistance or assistance rescues you.

In the end, your ultimate value in life and in whatever circumstances you pursue hinges more on how you develop your character and become the real person you are now. As the ancient Greek philosopher, Aristotle, once wrote: *"The ultimate end in life depends upon awareness and the power of contemplation rather than upon mere survival."*

You should reflect how incapacitated and limited you become whenever you derive your everyday life decisions exclusively in your comfort zones. If you do not develop your ability for PMA, then you deprive yourself not only relishing on the greater possibilities of survival but also, basking on the enduring and larger satisfactions in life.

Practicing all these survival guidelines ensures you can achieve your intents in general and can alter your old self and thoughts to alter your way of life in particular. You can expect to live in the present day narrating the near-tragic tale of your courageous stand fighting cunningly for survival to all your friends and family, and someday, to the next generation with your grandchildren.

Reading the final canto will make you bid farewell to any doubt or woe. So, confront the challenges as you go. Create solutions, as you will now know; as ever, emerge with a healthy glow!

Enjoy reading throughout the pages! Earn to learn something priceless! Read on towards fruition… towards becoming a responsible person… towards valuing and living a hale and happy life filled with satisfaction!

"It is always much prudent to prepare and prevent rather than to repair and repent."

— **David Kennedy**

PSYCHOLOGICAL PREPARATION & PLANNING

"Preparation through education is less costly than learning through tragedy."

—**Max Mayfield,** American Director of the National Hurricane Center

Since time immemorial, humanity has always been able to survive several various shifts and thrive through evolutions and devolutions in the environment. The ability of humankind to adapt mentally and physically to a constantly changing world has kept humanity alive while other inferior species in the surroundings perished gradually.

These similar survival capacities and mechanisms, which aided our primeval ancestors to flourish through ages after ages, can help us to thrive along generations after generations as well! Nevertheless, if we are unable to learn and anticipate the presence of stresses midst our existence or survival, then these helpful mechanisms can also work against us.

Survival involves an elemental science of psychology. In a survival scenario, you experience a slew of stresses that will ultimately influence your mindset. Hence, it does not come as a surprise that any normal individual will undergo certain psychological or internal reactions in the midst of a survival scenario:

❖ **Anger & Frustration** – Hostile disposition usually coming from the annoyance at being thwarted in attaining survival goals

❖ **Fear & Anxiety** – Emotions anticipating some specific danger, pain, or suffering

❖ **Guilt & Depression** – Remorse resulting from feeling responsible for some loss; breeds a mental state, characterized by a despondent lack of activity and a pessimistic sense of inadequacy

❖ **Loneliness & Boredom** – Sadness brought about by being abandoned, forsaken, or in solitary isolation

These natural responses are actually stress factors. They can shape your inner emotions and thoughts. If you do not have a clear understanding of these stresses, then they can easily change your well-trained and confident character into an ineffective and indecisive person with dubious and unreliable abilities for survival.

For this reason, it is imperative at the outset of this manual to facilitate you towards a better understanding of the nature of these stresses. Besides, you will learn the ability to control yourself and developing your mental capacities in confronting real-world survival scenarios.

In effect, these stressors will create within you the impetus to function prudently and conduct yourself accordingly. You will even discover the much-needed motivation to work harder without any solicited advice or initiatives coming from anybody else suggesting to you what to do.

The knowledge you gain from this initial chapter will help you to prepare yourself to come through the toughest and harshest times alive. Without a will and mental capacity to survive, all your acquired survival skills serve little purpose; invaluable knowledge only goes down the drain.

STRESS STRENGTHS & SURVIVAL STRESSORS

This section will help you recognize and explain the distress or stresses of survival and transforming them into strengths. It further dwells on the stressors resulting from these stressful events.

Stress, per se, is not an illness that you cure and rule out. Instead, stress is an omnipresent condition we all experience. It can be either destructive or constructive; it can either discourage or encourage us; it can either stop us dead in our tracks or stir us moving forward. Summarily, stress can make life and our existence either seemingly meaningless or apparently meaningful.

Nonetheless, this manual describes stress as our psychological reaction, physical stimulus, and internal (emotional and spiritual) response to the pressures and tensions of life. Undeniably, we need stress since it creates for us several positive gains.

Foremost, stress bestows demanding challenges upon us. It provides us chances to know our worth, strengths, and values.

Stress can also manifest our ability to deal with pressure without crumbling down. Yet, stress can also induce us to panic and forget all of our survival knowledge and training.

It tests and proves our innate traits of flexibility and adaptability. As such, stress can stimulate us to work efficiently in the best way we can and know how in a survival scenario.

Since we do not usually consider insignificant events as stressful, then stress can be a perfect indicator of the importance we associate with a particular event. In short, stress plays up or highlights what is more valuable and important to us.

Indeed, we ought to have some sort of stress—or an element of it—in our lives. Yet, our intent is having it without any excesses; as the cliché goes, *'too much of anything is good for nothing, if not, injurious!'*

Excessive stress results in distress. As we all know, distress leads to uncomfortable tensions and psychological sufferings, which we oftentimes try to escape, or rather, avoid.

The following are just some of the most common indications of distress you and others may experience when confronted with excessive and unbearable stress:

- **Constant Doubting and Worrying**
- **Difficulties in Making Decisions**
- **Furious Flare-ups**
- **Heightened Tendencies of Forgetting**
- **Negligence and Carelessness**
- **Propensity for Committing Mistakes**
- **Perceptions about Suicide or Death**
- **Shying Away from Responsibilities**
- **Reduced Energy Levels**
- **Trouble of Building Good Relations with Others**
- **Withdrawing from, or Avoiding Others**

Therefore, the fundamental skill to your survival is the ability to handle the inevitable and impending stresses you will eventually experience. To be a survivor, you must work with your stresses rather than allowing your stresses work on you.

Any circumstance may lead to stress. As we have experienced, stressful events do not always occur one at a time; they oftentimes happen simultaneously. Such stress-producing events are what we call, *'survival stressors.'*

Survival stressors are the evident causes. Stress is obviously our reaction.

As soon as our body identifies the existence of a stressor, it then starts instinctively to react by protecting itself. This protective preparation involves transmitting an internal distress signal throughout our body.

Consequentially, our body will only know a couple of protective measures: it prepares to either *'fight or flee.'* While our body organs react to the distress signal, a series of organic responses actually take place in simultaneous fashion:

❖ **Enhanced Body Metabolism** – Breaking down large amounts of stored fuels (fats and carbohydrates or sugar) to boost adrenaline and provide energy

❖ **Rapid Breathing Rate** – Supplying more oxygen to the bloodstreams

❖ **Increased Blood Pressure and Heart Rate** – Providing more blood to the muscles

❖ **Heightened Muscle Tensions** – Preparing the body for action

- ❖ **Stimulated Blood-Clotting Mechanisms** – Reducing bleeding from open cuts and wounds

- ❖ **Sharpened Sensory Faculties** – Enabling you to be more aware and alert of your surroundings

By this natural protective posture, it allows you to cope and deal with potential harm and injuries. However, you cannot maintain, much less, endure indefinitely such enhanced levels of alertness.

Stressors are discourteous! A stressor never goes away just because a new one sets in. Stressors accumulate. Hence, an accumulation of minor stressors can transform into a major distress.

Ultimately, as the sources of stress persist or increase, our resistance to stress erodes. Our body eventually reaches a state of exhaustion. At this instance, our ability to defy stress or exploit it to our favor passes out. Subsequently, signs of distress appear.

In this regard, the two principal factors for effective stress management have the ability to anticipate stressors and formulate strategies to cope with these stressors. Thus, it is essential that you must also be aware of the following common types of real possible stressors you have to face in a survival scenario:

- ❖ **Environmental Setting**

- ❖ **Illnesses, Injuries, or Death**

- ❖ **Loss of Energy or Fatigue**

- ❖ **Separation or Isolation**

- ❖ **Thirstiness & Hungriness**

❖ Uncertainties & Control Deficiencies

Although all these survival stressors can be stressful to you, bear in mind that each of them does not have similar stressful effects on other people. Each of us responds differently to these stressors. Your prior training, experiences, mental and physical conditioning, self-confidence level, and outlook in life contribute largely to what you will determine as stressful in a survival scenario.

As a review, your main objective is not to escape or avoid stress. Instead, you must learn to manage these survival stressors by making them work to your advantage.

Mental Motivation: Alertness, Aptitude, and Awareness

Survival is never exclusive to recognizing its stresses, learning about its stressors or acquiring the basic survival skills and training. More importantly, survival concerns motivating yourself and training your focus towards coming through alive.

Motivation initiates to inspire, guide, and maintain your survival-oriented objectives and attitude. It is what stimulates you to take action towards your survival goals.

Therefore, motivation is the reason for and behind your course of action, which gives purpose and direction to your attitude. Essentially, your motivation to survive involves a comprehensive preparation to your psyche.

Key aspects of this mental preparation include improvements in your alertness, inherent abilities, and awareness. All these personal enhancements ensure productive reactions in a survival scenario.

Keep in mind that survival is natural and instinctive to all; circumstances thrusting you unexpectedly into a struggle between life and death survival is unnatural. Hence, never fear your natural reactions to this unnatural spot.

You only need to prepare yourself subjugating these reactions in serving your ultimate goal—staying alive and giving more meaning to your life and existence. Numerous nuances of self-sacrifice, courage, and heroism had emerged from the challenge of survival.

You can unveil all these virtuous qualities of the human spirit in you, especially if you prepare yourself psychologically for survival. Here are some of the more significant guidelines to prepare your mentality and survival attitude:

❖ **Rediscover Your Real Person** – Amidst your interactions with your family and intimate circles, take the time to reflect and know your real self on the inside. Make your strengths stronger and develop the qualities that you know are favorable and necessary for survival.

❖ **Identify and Anticipate Your Fears** – Never pretend that you bear no fears. Start imagining about what truly frightens you if forced to survive by your lonesome. Train yourself in those fears. Your goal is not to get rid of your fear, but to grow the confidence in your abilities to function despite all your fears.

❖ **Adopt and Embrace a Positive Mental Attitude** – Learn to see the positivity and potential benefits in everything. Positivism not only boosts your morale but also, excellently stimulates your common sense and ingenuity.

❖ **Practice Being Realistic** – Never worry when making an honest assessment of situations. Visualize the circumstances as the way they are, and never as something you wish them to be. Confine your expectations and hopes within the realistic appraisal of the situation.

Going into a survival scenario with unrealistic expectations will surely lay the groundwork for resentful disappointments and cynicism. Subscribe to the maxim, *'Hope for the best; prepare for the worst!'* As always, it would be much easier for you adjusting to pleasant surprises arising from your unexpected serendipities than feeling upset by your unexpected cruel circumstances.

❖ **Admonish Your Psyche on the Real Risks and Issues** – Know that the failure to undergo psychological preparations in dealing with survival leads to reinforcing those aforementioned internal reactions and stress factors. As a result, you give up even before your body gives in. Remember, at stake is your life, as well as the lives of others who rely on you to perform responsibly your part.

❖ **Acquire Stress Management Skills** – In all probabilities, you panic easily, especially when you are under stress and you do not have the proper training or psychological preparations to challenge whatever crises may occur, wherever and whenever. Although we cannot usually control the survival scenarios we may find ourselves in, it is clearly within our abilities to control our reactions to these survival circumstances.

Developing your stress management skills can improve significantly your capability of staying calm at all times. Your calmness allows you to focus more on working to keep yourself (and others) surviving through the ordeal.

A few basic stress management skills and techniques you must learn include cognitive restructuring (or the ability to ascertain and see a situation, assertiveness, time management, and relaxation. Have a clear understanding that the *'will to survive'* can also mean interchangeably as the *'refusal to give up.'*

S.P.E.A.R. / S.U.R.V.I.V.A.L. Systems

Coming through a difficult situation obviously implies encountering one challenge after another while avoiding panic. When thrust into these possible scenarios, set to *'S.P.E.A.R.'* the situation:

- ❖ S—Stop
- ❖ P—Plan
- ❖ E—Execute
- ❖ A—Assess
- ❖ R—Re-evaluate

By S.P.E.A.R., you address systematically the survival scenario prior to implementing your basic survival skills. This survival system will help you to focus your body and frame of mind to avoid shaping negative mindsets and other overwhelming feelings of fear and anxiety.

Alternatively, you may develop your own survival pattern, which enables you to conquer the adversaries and obstacles of survival. Your survival pattern must include—in order of necessity vis-à-vis the nature of the environment—shelter, water, food, fire, first aid, and SOS signals.

It is, however, imperative to alter your survival pattern as the environment changes. As a rule of thumb, establish in your mind the exigency of a survival pattern in order to meet and satisfy your immediate physical necessities based on the scenario.

This manual shares the survival pattern adopted by the Department of the Army of the U.S.A. It encapsulates wittily the corresponding letters forming the word 'S.U.R.V.I.V.A.L.' Each letter denotes a guide on how to direct your actions and approaches in any survival scenario (refer to Image-1).

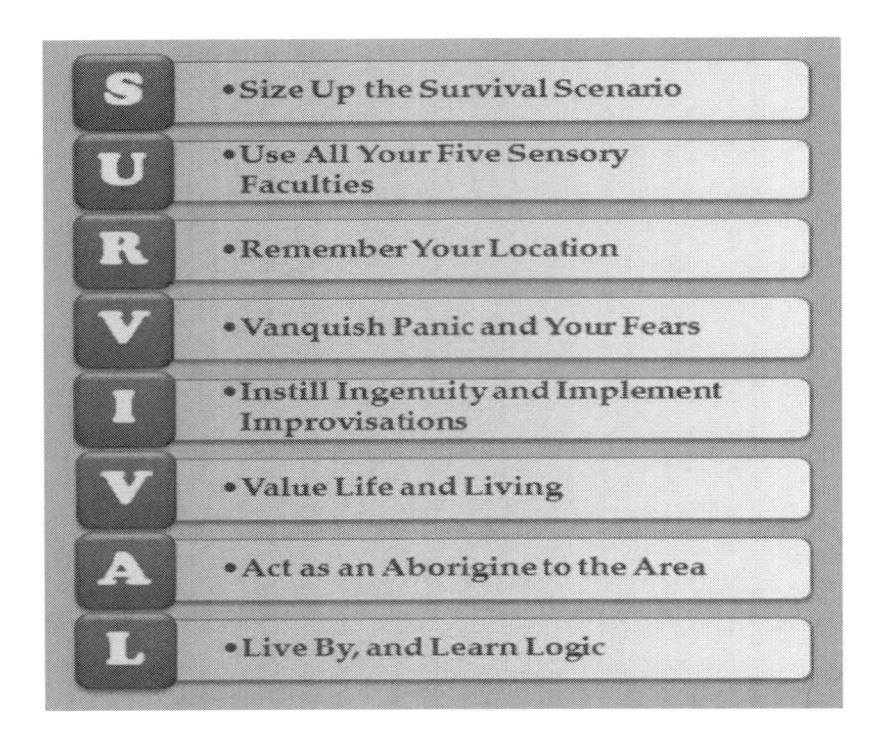

S	• Size Up the Survival Scenario
U	• Use All Your Five Sensory Faculties
R	• Remember Your Location
V	• Vanquish Panic and Your Fears
I	• Instill Ingenuity and Implement Improvisations
V	• Value Life and Living
A	• Act as an Aborigine to the Area
L	• Live By, and Learn Logic

S—Size Up the Survival Scenario: Before making any decisions and taking actions, obtain a general familiarization of the situation—surroundings, physical condition, and survival supplies and equipment. You will also have to consider scrutinizing what the ensuing circumstances on the survival scenario are when you create and implement your survival plan.

U—Use All Your Five Sensory Faculties: Apply all your senses (i.e., seeing, hearing, smelling, tasting, and feeling) when considering all the aspects of the scenario. Take stock of the sights, sounds, and smells. Raise your sensitivities to certain temperature changes. Always be observant.

Plan your actions. You may make a misstep when you respond quickly without analyzing or planning. Remember, *'undue haste makes waste.'* Such blunders may cause further jeopardy, if not, death.

Hence, never act in haste or for the sake of making a move. Otherwise, the situation disorients you until you will no longer know what to do, or where to go.

R—Remember Your Location: Focus on where you are, as well as where you are going. When you have a companion, never rely on your companion/s to keep track of your location and route.

You should constantly orient yourself. At the least, keep on determining how your current spot relates to other important locations such as local water and food sources, including areas that will provide subsistence.

If you have a map, refer to your location and relate it to the terrains surrounding you. This is a fundamental orienteering principle that you must ever heed.

V—Vanquish Panic and Your Fears: Fear and panic are the most overwhelming obstacles in a survival scenario. You should circumvent or surmount them.

If you cannot control both emotions, fear and panic can ruin your ability to make intelligent decisions. They can create more stresses by letting you react to your imaginations and emotions instead of responding to your situation.

I—Instill Ingenuity and Implement Improvisations: Learning to improvise can save your life. The concept of improvisation is to figure out other applications you can make and use out of a certain tool designed for a particular purpose.

You must learn using natural objects around you for various needs and intents. A fine example is using a rock as a hammer.

A complete survival kit may be essential; but, the supplies can run out and the instruments may wear out after a short while. Your creative imagination and resourcefulness shall then take over after depleting your survival kit, or even without it.

V—Value Life and Living: Every birth of humanity involves a struggle to live. However, all of us have grown into the habit of living through the comforts and softer sides of life. We abhor discomforts, hardships, and inconveniences.

What then befalls upon us, or what shall be the supreme issue to weigh, when a survival scenario— replete with its discomforts, inconveniences, and stresses—is at hand? Apparently, putting a premium on living—or *'the will to live'*—becomes vital.

The knowledge, training, and experiences you have acquired through life will have a collective bearing and significant relevance on your will to live. Your stubbornness, or your resolute refusal to submit yourself to the obstacles and issues that confront you, will provide you with the mental, emotional, physical, and spiritual strengths to hold out and endure.

A—Act as an Aborigine to the Area: Regional animals and natives have long adapted to their environment and ecosystem. Act as if you are one of them. Adapt to their way of living.

To get a hang of the area, become a keen observer on how the local animals and/or people handle earthly and mundane matters as they go about their usual routines. Learn what they eat and where to source their water and food.

Know how they use available resources for their subsistence. Animal life, which has necessities of water, food, and shelter analogous with humans, can readily offer you clues and essential indications on how to survive.

L—Live By, and Learn Logic: Logical learning in living and valuing life includes learning the basic survival skills. Equipping yourself with survival skills can influence your determination to survive in whatever scenario you find yourself in.

This means that you need to recognize the character of the survival setting or environment and apply your skills geared aptly to that survival scenario. For instance, you should know how and where to source water when the survival scenario is a desert.

"Do what you can with what you have got wherever you are."

—Theodore Roosevelt, 26th President of the United States

HUMAN HEALTH ESSENTIAL ELEMENTS

"Self-preservation is the first principle of our nature."

—**Alexander Hamilton**, American political leader and one of the founding fathers of the United States

Medical problems are among the multifarious issues that can impair a survivor's ability to return to safety. Generally, these medical conditions arise from injury-causing accidents, extreme climates, and an array of illnesses contracted while struggling for survival.

Many survivors will feel apathy with their difficulties in treating these medical issues amidst their survival scenarios. These feelings of helplessness usually stem from their deficiencies in emergency training (knowledge of <u>basic first aid</u>) and medical supplies.

Thus, it is always practical to acquire substantial information not only on the basic medical emergency responses but also, on the available environmental resources that have certain medical applications. Your ability to treat yourself and others will boost your morale and fighting power while making a great difference in your life and the lives of others.

You must know what to do to stay alive, even without any qualified medical persons around. However, to realize that responsibility is to learn first the essential elements of the human health.

The "Thriving Three's Tenets"

Foremost, learn the basic parameters for a human being to survive. These are parametric quantities, termed in this manual as the *Thriving Three's Tenets,* proclaiming that a human can survive and thrive under the following:

- ❖ **3 Minutes without Air**
- ❖ **3 Hours without a Regulated Body Temperature**
- ❖ **3 Days without Water**
- ❖ **3 Weeks without Food**

The importance of learning this survival doctrine is providing you with a guideline on prioritizing which of the most essential survival skills to apply primarily. In whatever survival scenario, the typical order would be setting up a shelter, sourcing out water, and foraging for food.

However, when disaster strikes and leaves you or your companions with physical damage (i.e., injuries and trauma), responding to medical emergencies should be immediate and paramount. Never forego facilitating first-aid treatment at a later period. Time is of the essence, just as the survival tenet prescribes.

MEDICAL MAINTENANCE

To survive while having a medical condition, you just need to remember three fundamental substantial sustenance or health maintenance requirements: water, food, and personal hygiene.

Substantial Sustenance # 1: Water

The human body drains water through certain normal body processes (i.e., defecation, urination, respiration, and perspiration). Illness, burns, high altitude, intense activity, and heat or cold exposure are other factors that can cause your body to lose more water.

The average human being loses about 2 to 3 liters of water daily during regular body exertions under a normal atmospheric temperature, which is at 20 °C (68 °F). Therefore, the body requires the same amount of water daily as a replacement.

When you replenish inadequately your lost body fluids, dehydration occurs. The most common signs and symptoms of dehydration are thirstiness, retarded refill of capillaries in fingernail beds, low urine output, loss of skin elasticity, fatigue, emotional instability, deepened line along the center of the tongue, darker and more odorous urine, and dark and sunken eyes.

By the time you crave for fluids, you are already 2 % dehydrated. In effect, dehydration reduces your ability to function efficiently. When injured, it heightens your susceptibility to intense shock.

Take into account the following consequences of body fluid loss (refer to Image-2).

Body Fluid Loss Percentage	Consequences
5 %	weakness or lethargy, thirst, nausea, and irritability
10 %	tingling sensation in the limbs, inability to walk, headache, and dizziness
15 %	swollen tongue, painful urination, numb feelings in the skin, dimmed vision, and deafness
more than 15 %	may result in death

The idea is to always replace your body fluids as you lose them. However, thirst is not an indicator of how much liquid you need.

It could be difficult trying to make up for a water deficit in a survival scenario. Most people cannot drink comfortably more than a liter of water at a time. Hence, even when you are not feeling thirsty, drink water in small amounts at regular intervals within each hour to avoid dehydration.

Of all the physical issues you may confront in a survival scenario, water loss is the most preventable. The following is your guide to prevent dehydration (refer to Image-3).

In any situation where food intake is low, drink 6 to 8 liters of water/day.
You consume water to aid your digestion process; so, always drink water when eating.
Acclimatize. When acclimatized, your body performs more efficiently under extreme conditions.
Conserve sweat; not water. Limit sweat-producing activities.
Ration water. Apportion your water supply sensibly until you find suitable sources. A daily intake of 0.5 liter of a sugar-water mixture (2 teaspoons/liter) will suffice to prevent severe dehydration for at least a week, provided you keep water losses to a minimum by limiting activity and heat loss or gain.
If you are experiencing severe conditions of mental or physical stress, increase your water intake. In principle, drink enough liquids so you keep up a minimum urine output of 0.5 liter/day.
In an extreme climate, especially an arid one, you can lose 2.5 to 3.5 liters of water/hour. Therefore, you should drink 14 to 30 liters of water/day.

As your body loses water, it also corresponds to a loss of body salts or *electrolytes*. Your regular diet can usually cope with these losses.

However, during an illness or an extreme situation, you need to provide additional liquid sources. To provide a salt-concentration liquid intake that your body tissues can absorb readily, you can take a salt-liquid mixture of 0.25 teaspoon of salt to a liter of water.

You have two options to determine the amount of fluid loss in your body. One is the *'body fluid-soaked garment method.'* Second is using the *'pulse and breathing rate method.'* Confer to the following as your guide (refer to Image-4).

BODY FLUID-SOAKED GARMENT METHOD	
GARMENT TYPE	BODY FLUID RETENTION
Standard Apparel	0.25 liter of blood
T-Shirt	0.5 to 0.75 liter of sweat
PULSE AND BREATHING RATE METHOD		
PULSE RATE	BREATHING RATE	BODY FLUID LOSS
100 beats/minute	12 to 20 breaths/minute	0.75 liter
100 to 120 beats/minute	20 to 30 breaths/minute	0.75 to 1.5 liters
120 to 140 beats/minute	30 to 40 breaths/minute	1.5 to 2 liters

NOTE: Vital signs above these rates require care that is more advanced.

Substantial Sustenance # 2: Food

While you can live for a number of weeks without any food intake, you just really need sufficient amounts to remain healthy. Without food, you become weak, and your body's functionalities will deteriorate quickly.

Food provides you with minerals, vitamins, salts, and other essential elements to good health. It replenishes those substances, which your body burns for energy.

Plants and animals, including fish, are the two basic food sources. In certain extents, both provide the macronutrients (i.e., calories, fats, proteins, and carbohydrates), which our body needs to function.

A calorie is a measure of energy-producing potential that is equal to the amount of heat contained in foods. As our body oxidizes the food we take, it releases this energy to stimulate our body's functionalities. An average person requires at least 2,000 calories daily to function at the minimum level.

A sufficient consumption of fats, proteins, and carbohydrates, but with inadequate intake of calories, will result in starvation. In severe cases, it leads to the body's cannibalism of its own tissues for energy.

Substantial Sustenance # 3: Personal Hygiene

In whatever survival scenario, cleanliness is an all-important factor to prevent diseases and infections. Poor personal hygiene can lessen your chances of survival.

An ideal proper hygiene is taking a daily shower with soap and hot water. However, you can remain clean without such indulgence. Wash your whole body with soapy water and a clean cloth. Focus washing on your hair, crotch, armpits, hands, and feet since these are primary areas prone to infection and infestation.

When having a scarcity of water, you can take an *'air bath.'* Strip off as much of your garments as practical; and then, expose your body to the air and sun for at least an hour. Just be careful not to acquire sunburn.

If you do not have soap, then use sand or ashes as a substitute. Alternatively, you can make soap out of animal fats and wood ashes (refer to Image-5).

> ### SOAP-MAKING FORMULA
> *(Animal Fat & Wood Ashes)*
>
> 1. Cut the animal fat into small pieces. Cook them in a pot to extract the grease.
>
> 2. Pour enough water to the pot to keep the fat from sticking while it cooks. Cook the fat slowly, stirring frequently.
>
> 3. After rendering the fat, pour the grease into a container to harden.
>
> 4. Place wood ashes in another container with a spout near the base.
>
> 5. Pour water over the ashes. Collect the liquid dripping out of the spout in a separate container. This liquid is the potash or lye. (Another method to get the lye is by pouring the slurry—ashes and water mixture—through a cloth that serves as a strainer.)
>
> 6. In a cooking pot, mix two parts grease to one part potash.
>
> 7. Place the pot over a fire. Boil the mixture until it thickens.
>
> 8. After the mixture—the soap—cools, you can use it in the semiliquid state directly from the pot. You can also pour it into a pan, allow it to harden, and cut it into bars for later use.

The following are other important aspects that you must pay attention to maintaining cleanliness:

❖ **Dental Care** – Brush your teeth and clean your mouth thoroughly at least once a day. If you do not have a toothbrush, then source out a chewing stick—some twig about 1 centimeter wide and 20 centimeters long that you chew on one end to separate the fibers and form into a brush.

You can also wrap around your fingers a clean strip of cloth, with which you rub your teeth. Another practical method is brushing your teeth with small amounts of salt, sand, soap, or baking soda. For your mouthwash, you can use either salt water or tea made from the willow bark.

As for your dental floss, any clean fiber or string can be a great substitute. If you have a tooth cavity, fill it temporarily with any of the following: candle wax, crushed aspirin tablet, ground ginger root or hot pepper, tobacco, and toothpaste.

❖ **Cleaning Clothing** – Keep your beddings and garments as clean as possible to avoid acquiring skin infections and parasitic infestations. If you have a deficient water supply, perform 'air cleaning' by airing and sunning your clothing for a couple of hours. If you are using a sleeping bag, make it a habit turning it inside out after every use; and then, fluff it up for airing.

❖ **Campsite Maintenance** – Human wastes must not soil your bivouac. Perform their dispositions far away from your campsite. With an unavailability of latrines, dig a *'cat hole'* for your wastes and cover it. Do not collect your drinking water downstream from your shelter site; else, purify all your water.

Part of healthy living and keeping you going is getting sufficient rest. Plan a regular rest period with at least 10 minutes/hour midst your daily routines.

Always learn to make yourself stress-free and relaxed under less than comfortable living conditions. A shift from a physical to a mental activity, or vice versa, can be pleasantly refreshing, especially when the situation or time does not allow you total relaxation.

Health maintenance is your systematic program of procedures to prevent illness, maintain maximum body function efficiencies, and promote health. It is central to your general health care and wellness, especially in all patterns—acute, chronic, episodic, preventive, and catastrophic.

"Man can live about forty days without food, about three days without water, about eight minutes without air, but only for one second without hope."

—**Charles Darwin**, British biologist, geologist, and naturalist

FIRST-AID FACILITATION

"Take some time to learn first aid and CPR. It saves lives and it works. Whether you are in a minor situation or something more serious, your knowledge of first aid will give you the confidence to act. You could be the difference between life and death!"

—**Bobby Sherman**, American singer-songwriter

First aid is the immediate assistance you give to yourself, or any person, suffering from a sudden injury or illness. The essential procedure of performing first aid includes the initial life-saving intervention in a state of emergency.

This swift preliminary action involves the application of basic medical skills training—performing mouth-to-mouth or cardiopulmonary resuscitation (CPR), plastering a cut, splinting, etc.—and any available complete or partial treatment prior to seeking professional medical assistance or awaiting rescue operations.

In summary, the primary intent of first aid is to provide care in order to preserve life; prevent the condition from worsening; and eventually, promote a quick recovery. Briefly, this summation of objectives comprises what the medical field termed as *'The Three Ps of First Aid'*(refer to Image-6).

Preserve Life

It could be your life or other's. The main responsibility of a first responder is to preserve life of the injured person by providing first aid treatments. The first responder should start the first aid procedures of DR. ABC:

Danger – evaluate the emergency scene for further danger.
Respond – exercise a quick response to assist.
Airway – ensure that the victim has an airway.
Breathing – ensure that the person is breathing.
Circulation – examine the quality of the respiratory circulation.

If necessary, perform CPR and rescue breathing until medical professionals arrive.

Prevent Deterioration

The responder must keep the patient stable and reassure that the condition must not worsen before medical emergency assistance or rescue operators arrive. At this point, the main responsibilities of a first responder must provide a safe and comfortable position to the casualty, prevent further injury, and apply further first aid techniques.

Promote Recovery

Following the first aid treatment, the responder should encourage confidence in the patient, attempt to relieve pain, and take steps that may help in the recovery process.

Expediting Emergencies

Various medical emergencies, clinical conditions, and health problems can abound in any survival scenario. When performing a quick emergency response, you must control the panic of the victim and your own.

Perform a quick physical exam and look for the root cause of the issue. Thereafter, resolve the situation by following the ABCs or the Three Ps of First Aid.

Nevertheless, always be discerning and exercise prudence. In some cases, an individual can die more quickly due to arterial bleeding than from an obstructed airway.

This manual dwells on the following most common emergencies to expedite: breathing issues; open or infected wounds; shock or severe bleeding; bone, joint, and muscle injuries; animal bites and stings; skin diseases; and, environmental ailments;

Breathing Issues

Stopped breathing and other respiratory difficulties are direct results of an obstructed airway caused by any of the following factors:

➢ Mouth or throat swelling, or inflammation due to an allergic reaction or the inhalation of smoke, fumes, and irritating vapors

➢ Neck or facial injuries

➢ Painful neck spasm (kink), which results in an angulation, twisting, or bending of the neck forward and resting the chin on the chest

➢ Presence of foreign matter in the mouth or throat

➢ An unconscious condition, whereby, the lower jaw muscles tend to relax and drop the neck forward, prompting the tongue to drop back

TECHNICAL TREATMENT:

✚ Check whether the patient has a completely or partially obstructed airway. When the patient has a completely blocked airway, or when the patient's neck bends forward, perform *'opening the airway maneuverings'* by either the *'head tilt-chin lift method'* or *'jaw thrust method'* (refer to Image-7A & 7B).

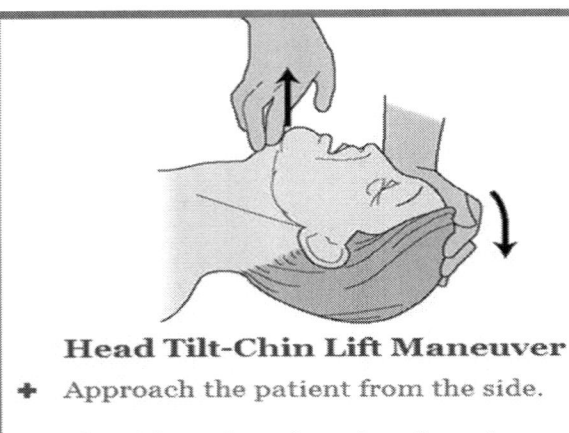

Head Tilt-Chin Lift Maneuver

✚ Approach the patient from the side.

✚ Place the palm of one hand on the patient's forehead and push down gently, rolling the patient's head towards the top.

✚ Using the fingers of your free hand, lift lightly the chin even further up.

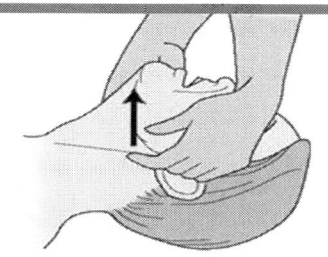

> **Jaw Thrust Maneuver**
> + Approach the patient facing the top of the head.
> + Place both of your hands on each side of the face, with your thumbs on the cheek bone while your fingertips are underneath the jaw bone.
> + Pull the lower jaw forward by lifting your fingers while pushing down slightly with your thumbs. Alternatively, for more force and stability, you can use your palms to push down on the cheeks as you lift the jawbone.
> + If the patient's lips are closed, open the lower lip with your thumb.

✚ You can also perform abdominal thrusts until clearing the airway. Alternatively, by using your finger, you can sweep quickly the patient's mouth clear of any foreign matters

✚ If the patient has a partially blocked airway, which implies that the victim can speak or manage a cough, then simply allow clearing the obstruction naturally.

✚ When the victim is unconscious, administer a CPR procedure (refer to Image-8).

CPR is as easy as C-A-B

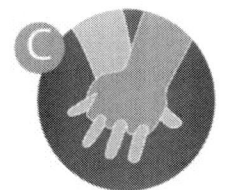

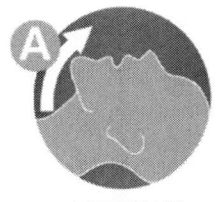

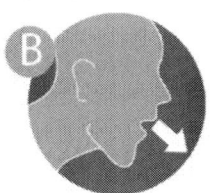

COMPRESSIONS | **AIRWAY** | **BREATHING**

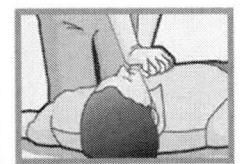

Push hard at least 2 inches on the patient's breastbone, 100x/minute to circulate oxygenated blood to the body's vital organs.

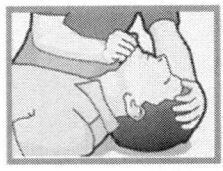

Tilt the patient's head and lift the chin back to open the airway. Check for breathing or blockage; observe the rise and fall of the chest. Listen for any air movement.

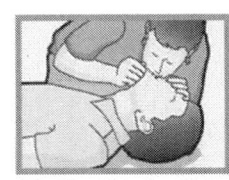

Tilt the chin back for the unobstructed passage of air; give mouth-to-mouth rescue breaths, and then, resume those hard-and fast chest compressions.

NOTE: *The newly revised 2015 CPR guideline of the American Heart Association (AHA) emphasizes the importance of starting immediately chest compressions instead of opening the airway and breathing into the mouth of the patient first; BUT, the new CPR procedures only becomes secondary to controlling any occurrence of severe or intense bleeding.*

Open & Infected Wounds and Cuts

Wounds characterize an interruption in the integrity or normal continuity of the skin. The typical survival scenario wounds are either open or infected and include other skin diseases.

Open Wounds

In a survival scenario, open wounds can cause serious concerns since they do not only damage tissues or result in excessive blood loss but also, they are prone to infections. Bacteria present on the object inflicting the wound, on the patient's clothing and skin, or on other foreign matters touching the wound can lead to infection.

TECHNICAL TREATMENT:

✚ The principle for treating open wounds is to reduce further contamination right from the start. Perform the proper *'wound cleaning procedures'* as soon as it occurs (refer to Image-9).

> **Wound Cleaning Procedures**
>
> ➢ Remove clothing or cut it away from the wound.
>
> ➢ Find an exit wound, especially when a sharp object, projectile, or gunshot caused the wound.
>
> ➢ Clean thoroughly the skin surfaces around the wound.
>
> ➢ Rinse (but never scrub) the wound with running water. Gushing forth the open wound with fresh urine is applicable if water is unavailable.

✚ Never attempt closing any wound by performing suturing procedures. The safest means to manage a wound is to apply the *'open treatment method'* (refer to Image-10).

Open Treatment Method

➢ Leave the wound open to enable draining of the pus caused by infection.

➢ Cover the wound with a clean cloth to serve as a protective dressing and place a bandage on the cloth to hold it firmly in place.

➢ Change the dressing daily to check for further infection.

➢ If the wound is a gaping cut, you can bring its edges together with an adhesive tape (cut in the shape of a dumbbell or butterfly) and place it crosswise rather than along its length, as shown.

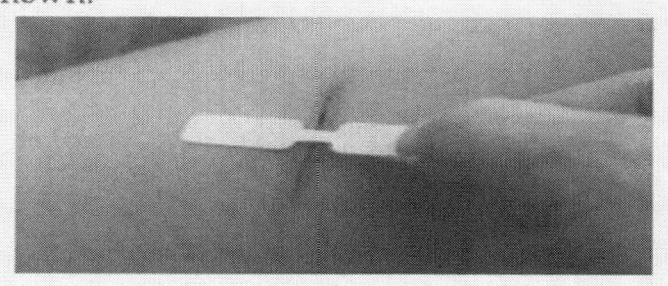

Image-10: Open Treatment Method with Butterfly Closure Strip Application

Infected Wounds

Certain extents of wound infections are inevitable in a survival scenario. A presence of infection manifests swelling, pain, pus, redness, and a burning sensation around the wound.

TECHNICAL TREATMENT:

✢ As a general treatment for an infected wound, apply the *'warm compress method'* (refer to Image-11).

Warm Compress Method

➢ Place a warm, moist compress directly on the infected wound. Keep the warm compress on the wound for 30 minutes. Change the compress when it cools.

➢ Drain the wound. Open and gently probe the infected wound with a sterile instrument.

➢ Dress and bandage the wound. Drink a lot of water.

NOTE: *Apply this procedure three or four times daily. Continue this treatment daily until all signs of infection have disappeared.*

Image-11: Warm Compress Method Application for Infected Wounds

✚ If the wound seems not to heal, turns severely infected, and antibiotics are unavailable or a simple *debridement* (surgical removal of dead tissues and contaminants in the wound) is impossible, consider performing the *'maggot therapy,'* despite its risks (refer to Image-11).

> **Maggot Therapy**
>
> ➤ Expose the wound to flies for one day, and then cover it.
>
> ➤ Check daily for maggots. As soon as the maggots develop, keep the wound covered, but check daily.
>
> ➤ Remove all the maggots when they have cleaned out all the dead tissues before they start picking on healthy tissues. Increased pain and bright red blood in the wound indicate that the maggots have reached a healthy tissue.
>
> ➤ Flush the wound repeatedly with sterile water or fresh urine to remove the maggots.
>
> ➤ Check the wound every four hours for several days to ensure the removal of all the maggots.
>
> ➤ Bandage the wound and treat it as any other wound. It should heal normally.

Image-12: The Maggot Debridement Therapy (MDT) Application for Infected Wounds

Burns & Scalds

A burn is an injury produced typically by heat, fire, electricity, radiation, or a caustic chemical agent. The term *'burn'* is an emphasis of the burning sensation denoting this injury. It characterizes severe skin damage that causes the death of skin cells.

TECHNICAL TREATMENT:

First Aid Treatment for Burns

➤ Stop the burning process as soon as possible. This may mean removing the person from the area, dousing flames with water or sand, or smothering the flames with a blanket or by rolling on the ground.

➤ Remove any clothing or jewelry near the burnt area of skin, including babies' nappies. However, do not try to remove anything that is stuck to the burnt skin as this could cause more damage.

➤ Cool the burn with cool or lukewarm running water for 20 minutes, as soon as possible after the injury. Never use ice, iced water, or any creams or greasy substances such as butter. For burns caused by white phosphorous, pick out the white phosphorous with tweezers; do not douse with water.

➤ Keep the patient warm. Use a blanket or layers of clothing, but avoid putting them on the injured area. Keeping warm will prevent hypothermia, where the body temperature drops below 35°C (95°F).

➤ Cover the burn with cling film. Put the cling film in a layer over the burn, rather than wrapping it around a limb. You can use a clean clear plastic bag for burns on your hand.

➤ Treat a burn as an open wound. Treat the pain from a burn with paracetamol or ibuprofen. Never give aspirin to children under 16 years of age. For facial burns, consider using morphine.

➤ Alternatively, soak dressings or clean rags for 10 minutes in a boiling tannic acid solution (obtained from tea, inner bark of hardwood trees, or acorns boiled in water). Cool the dressings or clean rags and apply over burns.

Image-13: First Aid Treatment for Burns & Scalds

Severe & Intense Bleeding

Severe bleeding is extremely dangerous, especially when blood gushes from any principal blood vessel of the body. You must control the bleeding immediately since replacement fluids are usually unavailable and the patient can die within a short span of minutes.

A 1-liter loss of blood produces moderate symptoms of shock. A 2-liter loss of blood produces a severe state of shock and endangers the body. A 3-liter or more blood loss is usually fatal.

Technical Treatment:

You can quickly control external bleeding by the following treatment applications: direct and indirect pressure, elevation, digital ligation, or tourniquet.

✚ **Direct Pressure** – is the most effective treatment application to control external bleeding. You apply pressure directly and firmly over the wound by using your hands while maintaining firm pressure long enough to secure against further blood leakage.

If bleeding continues after having applied direct pressure for 30 minutes, apply a pressure dressing. This dressing consists of a thick dressing of gauze or other suitable material applied directly over the wound and held in place with a tightly wrapped bandage (refer to Image-14).

David Kennedy

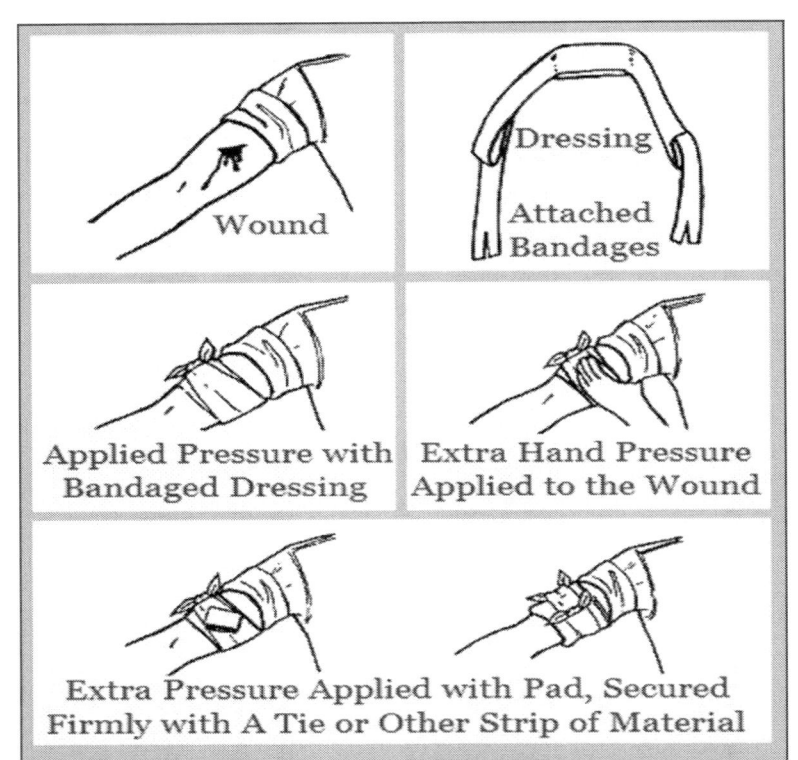

| Wound | Dressing Attached Bandages |
| Applied Pressure with Bandaged Dressing | Extra Hand Pressure Applied to the Wound |

Extra Pressure Applied with Pad, Secured Firmly with A Tie or Other Strip of Material

➢ The pressure dressing should be tighter than an ordinary compression bandage, but not so tight that it impairs the total circulation to the rest of the limb.

➢ Once applying the dressing, do not remove it, even when the dressing becomes blood-soaked. Leave the pressure dressing in place for 2 days, when you can then remove and replace it with a smaller dressing.

➢ In a long-term survival scenario, change the dressing daily and inspect for signs of infection.

Image-14

✚ **Elevation** – Elevating an injured limb as high as you can above the level of the heart will slow down blood loss. It also aids the return of blood flow to the heart while lowering the blood pressure in the region of the wound.

However, keep the limb lower than the heart when the injury comes from snakebites. Nonetheless, elevation alone does not control bleeding completely. Thus, you should also apply direct pressure over the wound at the same time.

✚ **Digital Ligation** – You can also impede major bleeding by using a finger or two to apply pressure over the bleeding vein's end. Retain the pressure until the bleeding slows down enough so you can apply a pressure dressing, limb elevation, and so forth.

✚ **Tourniquet** – Apply a tourniquet procedure only when no methods can control the bleeding. However, do not leave a tourniquet in place for too long; else, tissue damage can progress to gangrene, which can eventually result in the loss of the limb.

Improper tourniquet procedure application can also lead to permanent damage to the nerves and other tissues around the area of the constriction. When applying a tourniquet, situate it around the limb, between the heart and the wound, about 5 to 10 centimeters above the wound area (refer to Image-15).

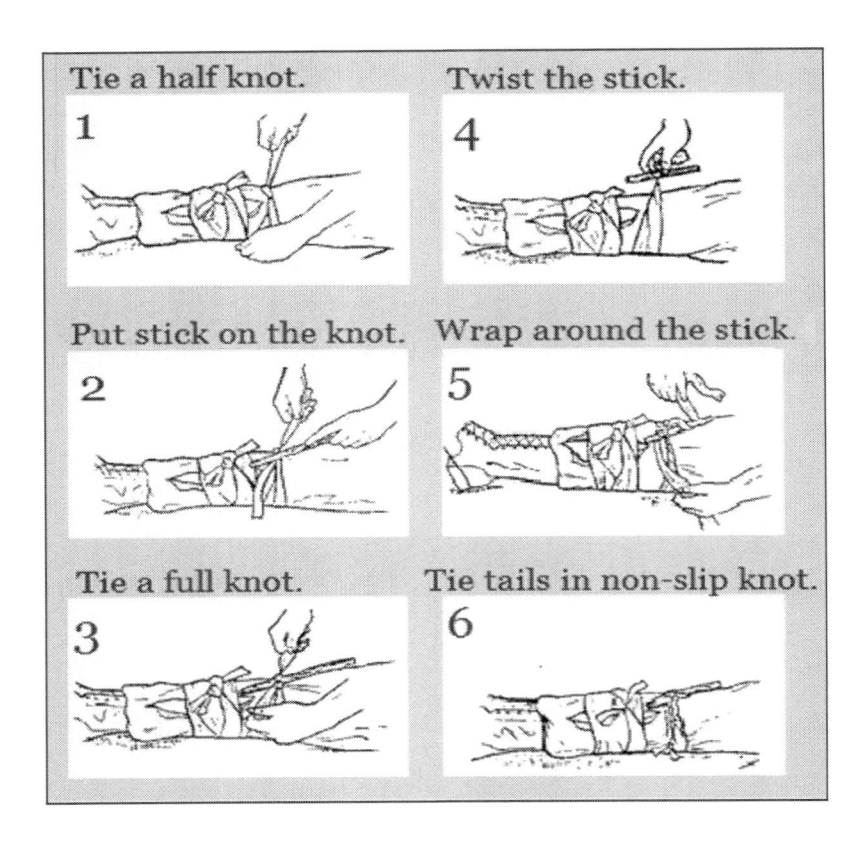

Image-15

Shock (Acute Stress Reaction)

Shock, per se, is not a disease; but rather, a clinical condition. It arises as a response to a traumatic or terrifying event, which induces strong emotional responses within a person. Symptoms of numbing or a sense of detachment manifest when an insufficiency of cardiac output fails filling the arteries with enough blood under pressure to provide adequate blood circulation to the body's organs and tissues.

TECHNICAL TREATMENT:

✚ Anticipate the occurrence of a shock to an injured individual. Regardless of whatever symptoms may appear, treat a shocked individual as follows (refer to Image-16).

CONSCIOUS PATIENT

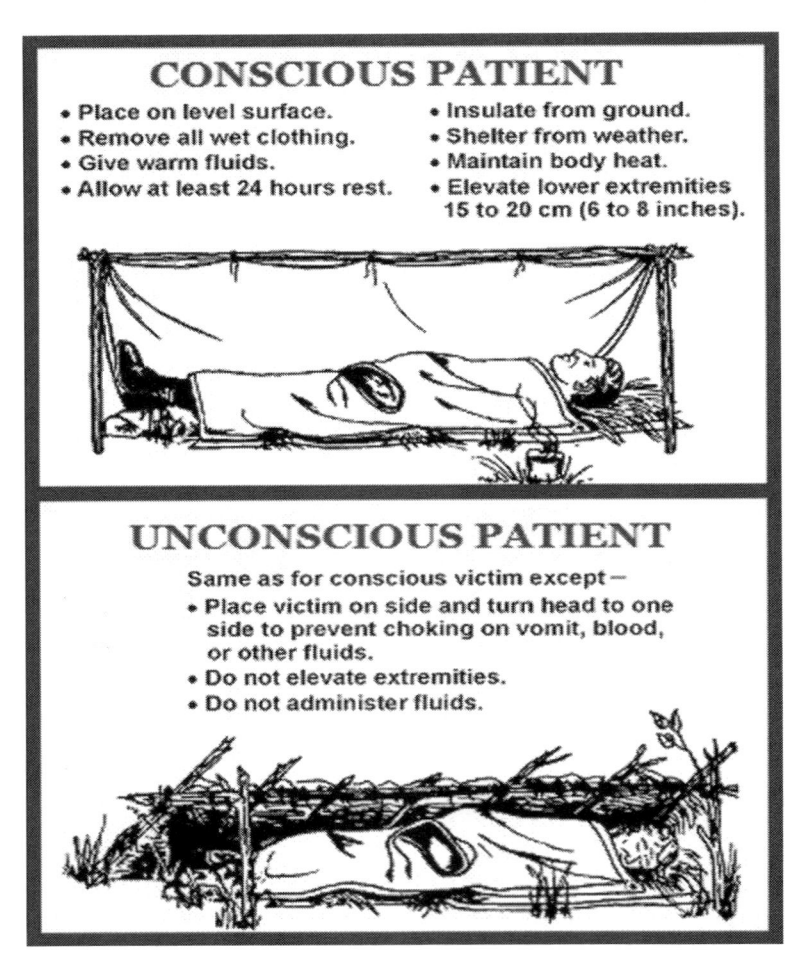

- Place on level surface.
- Remove all wet clothing.
- Give warm fluids.
- Allow at least 24 hours rest.
- Insulate from ground.
- Shelter from weather.
- Maintain body heat.
- Elevate lower extremities 15 to 20 cm (6 to 8 inches).

UNCONSCIOUS PATIENT

Same as for conscious victim except —
- Place victim on side and turn head to one side to prevent choking on vomit, blood, or other fluids.
- Do not elevate extremities.
- Do not administer fluids.

Image-16

Bone, Joint, and Muscle Injuries

The most common bone, joint, and muscle injuries, which concern both legs and arms, are fractures, dislocations, sprains, and bruises. For major injuries like a bone fracture or dislocation, you can only manipulate a minimum emergency intervention.

Bone Fracture & Dislocation

A fracture is a break in continuity or a crack in the bone. A dislocation is the separation of bone joints, causing an improper bone alignment.

There are two principal types of fractures—open and closed. An open or compound fracture denotes that the bone is protruding through the skin. With an open wound, it complicates further the actual fracture.

The closed fracture indicates no open wounds. Typically, the interior broken bones can rub together, giving rise to its signs and symptoms such as skin discoloration, pain, swelling deformity, tenderness, and loss of function of the affected limb.

Compressed or severed nerves (blood vessels) around the area of the fracture are considerably the dangerous aspect of the injury. This is the reason why you should only perform a very cautious and minimal first aid intervention.

TECHNICAL TREATMENT:

✣ **Immobilization** – Initially, follow the treatment guidelines for acute stress reaction to rest the patient and control any internal bleeding. Set immobilization procedures or fixating the position of the joint or fractured limb of the patient by using an improvised traction-splint device (refer to Image-17).

David Kennedy

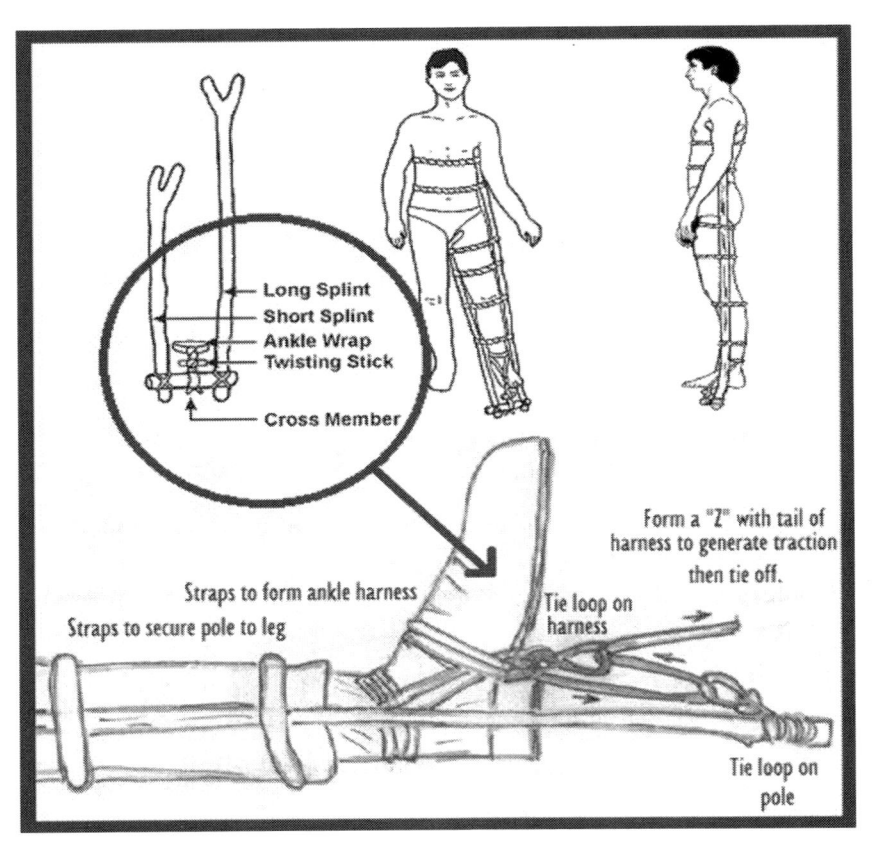

Image-17: Immobilization Procedure thru an Improvised Traction-Splint Device

✚ Traction – You must maintain traction or the application of a pulling force during the splinting and recovery process. You can pull effectively smaller bones like the lower leg or arm by hand.

✚ Setting or Reduction – A bone setting procedure places back forcefully the dislocated bones into their natural alignment. This is quite a more painful and complex treatment process. Hence, it is advisable to apply the easiest and safest traction technique of using weights in pulling or setting the bones.

✚ **Rehabilitation and Recovery** – After about a week or two, you can already remove the splints to prepare for rehabilitation. Let the patient function gradually by using the injured joint until recovering fully.

Sprains & Bruises

These are minor injuries, usually arising from an accidental overstretching of a ligament or tendon. However, they exhibit similar signs and symptoms of the major bone, joint, and muscle injuries.

TECHNICAL TREATMENT:

✚ You only have to remember the key letters—I.C.E.—for the treatment of sprains and bruises:

I.C. E. Treatment

➢ **I**ce the affected area for 24 hours; apply heat thereafter.

➢ **C**ompression dressing and/or splinting helps to stabilize.

➢ **E**levate the affected area.

Image-18: I.C.E. Treatment for Sprains & Bruises

Animal Stings and Bites

A plethora of animal species can sting or bite human beings. However, this manual covers the most commonly encountered stings and bites—insect bites, snakebites, spider bites, and scorpion stings—in any survival scenario.

An individual's reaction to animal stings and bites depends primarily on the amount and type of venom (if there are any), which injects into the animal's bite. Further typical responses imply whether the victim is allergic to the animal's venom and whether the stinging or biting animal carries a disease-causing agent.

Insect Bites

Insects and other related pests pose to be hazardous elements in any environment. Not only do they cause irritations but also, they are, generally, carriers of a host of diseases that often cause severe allergic and other hypersensitivity reactions in some people.

Your best option to avoid certain complications from insect stings and bites is to have updated immunization inoculations or vaccinations, which also includes provisions of booster shots. Alternatively, simply avoid insect-infested areas. Using netted fabrics for shelter and applying insect repellents are also helpful.

Whenever insects sting or bite you, never scratch the affected area since it might become infected. The following is a list of insects with their respective infectious diseases they transmit (refer to Image-19).

The Lost Ways

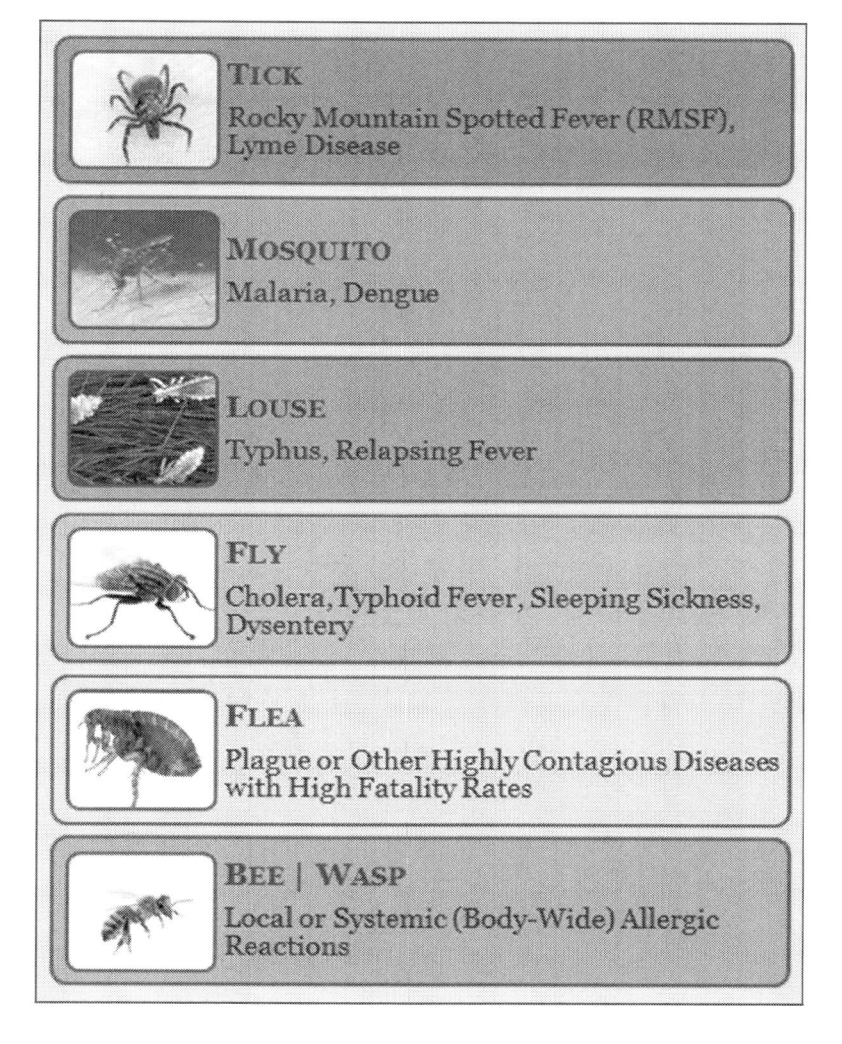

TICK
Rocky Mountain Spotted Fever (RMSF), Lyme Disease

MOSQUITO
Malaria, Dengue

LOUSE
Typhus, Relapsing Fever

FLY
Cholera, Typhoid Fever, Sleeping Sickness, Dysentery

FLEA
Plague or Other Highly Contagious Diseases with High Fatality Rates

BEE | WASP
Local or Systemic (Body-Wide) Allergic Reactions

Image-19

Technical Treatment:

It would be impossible to list specifically each treatment procedure for each type of insect stings and bites. The following will serve as your general treatment procedure (refer to Image-20).

Insect Sting & Bite Treatment

➤ Wash the sting site thoroughly with soap and water to lessen the chance of secondary infections.

➤ Relieve the discomfort and itching by applying any of the following: onion, dandelion sap, crushed garlic, cooling paste composed of ashes and mud, cold compress, or coconut meat.

➤ If you noticed ticks attached to your skin, cover them with either Vaseline™ (petroleum jelly) or oil, or certain tree saps. This will shut off their air supply. (Ticks release instinctively their hold without the presence of air; you can then remove them.) Clean the tick wound daily until healed.

➤ If stung by a bee or wasp, immediately remove the stinger and venom sac (if attached) by scraping with a knife blade or fingernail. Never grasp or squeeze the venom or stinger sac; else, it will force more venom into the wound.

Image-20: General Treatment Procedures for Insect Stings & Bites

Spider Bites & Scorpion Stings

Spiders and scorpions own varying extents of venom. Accordingly, their bites and stings also render varying symptoms.

However, their treatments are almost similar. Thus, it is vital to identify which specific species bit or stung to know its respective treatment (refer to Image-21).

BLACK WIDOW SPIDER
Facts: Mostly, its bite does not inject venom, except for those South American species.
Symptoms: Pain, bleeding, and infection
Treatment: Treat as an open wound. Similar treatment procedure to a Black Widow Spider bite when posioning occurs.

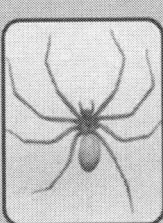

BROWN HOUSE SPIDER OR BROWN RECLUSE SPIDER
Facts: Its bite has little to no pain but a star-shaped, firm area of purplish discoloration appears at the bitten area.
Symptoms: Persistent ulcer that does not heal for weeks or months, fever, chills, joint pain, swollen lymph glands, vomiting, and rashes
Treatment: Treat as you would for shock and prepare performing CPR.

TARANTULA
Facts: Mostly, its bite does not inject venom, except for those South American species.
Symptoms: Pain, bleeding, and infection
Treatment: Treat as an open wound. Similar treatment procedure to a Black Widow Spider bite when posioning occurs.

SCORPION
Facts: It has a poisonous sting.
Symptoms: Pain and swelling around the stung area, prickly sensation around the mouth and a thick-feeling tongue, respiratory difficulties, body spasms, drooling, double vision, blindness, involuntary rapid eye movement, involuntary urination and defecation, and heart failure
Treatment: Similar treatment procedure to a Black Widow Spider bite.

Image-21: Facts, Symptoms, and Treatment for Spider Bites & Scorpion Stings

Snakebites

Deaths due to snakebites are quite rare. Nevertheless, snakebite possibilities in a survival scenario can affect morale. Thus, your failure to conduct preventive measures or failure to administer proper treatment of snakebites can lead to a needless tragedy.

Animal bite wounds, regardless of the species inflicting the injury, can worsen through infection stimulated by bacteria present in the animal's mouth. Yet, other snake fangs not only contain a multitude of bacteria but also, the deadly venom that destroys the blood circulation and central nervous system (CNS).

A snake's venom can result in extensive deaths of body tissues; and thus, leaving a prominently large open wound. Worse, without proper treatment, the injury could necessitate eventual amputation.

Panic, anxiety, and shock can further aggravate the recovery process of a victim bitten by a snake. Such hysteric emotions can actually hasten the circulation of the blood; and thereby, causing the victim's body to absorb the snake's toxins much quicker.

Indications of shock typically occur within half an hour after the bite. Prior to beginning treating snakebites, identify whether the snake was poisonous or not. You can determine the snake's vicious nature by looking at the appearance of its bite.

Bites inflicted by a nonpoisonous snake exhibit typically rows of teeth or bite marks. Although bites inflicted by a poisonous snake show a similar fashion, they distinctively have one or more puncture marks due to fang penetration.

Generally, the symptoms arising from a poisonous snakebite are the presences of immediate pains and swelling at the bitten area, blood in the urine, and spontaneous bleeding from the anus and nose. A couple of hours after the bite, the snake's neurotoxic venom triggers breathing difficulties, weakness, paralysis, weakness, numbness, and twitching.

TECHNICAL TREATMENT:

✚ **Nonpoisonous Snakebites** – Your chief concern in treating nonpoisonous snakebites is to confine the eventual destruction of the body tissues within the region of the bite. Irrigate the wound with clean running water and fresh air.

You can use a mild anti-bacterial soap to clean the wound. Avoid using strong antiseptics such as alcohol-based soaps and hydrogen peroxide. These substances can cause irritation and further damage to the healthy tissues.

Pat the wound dry with a soft, clean, and dry cloth instead of rubbing it dry to prevent further irritation. Treat the bite injury for <u>open wounds</u>.

✚ **Poisonous Snakebites** – Upon determining that the bite comes from a poisonous snake, perform the following procedures:

➢ Keep the victim still and give a reassurance. Remove all other constricting items from the victim's body (i.e., jewelry, watch, belt, tie, etc.).

➢ Clean the region of the bite, and prepare treatment procedures for a shock. If available, provide an antivenin intravenous (IV) injection.

➢ Open and maintain an airway, especially for bites on the facial surfaces. Prepare to administer CPR.

➢ Apply a constricting band (tourniquet) between the heart and wound. As a reminder, never raise a bitten limb above the level of the victim's heart.

➢ As soon as possible, extract the venom by squeezing the bite area or using a mechanical suction device through the following procedures:

➢ Make a careful incision—no more than 3 millimeters deep and no more than 6 millimeters long—over each of the bite punctures. Ensure that the incision only cuts through the skin's first or second layer. It must also be just deep enough to enlarge quite a bit the wound's opening.

➢ Secure a suction cup and place it over the bite area until creating an effective vacuum seal. Suction the wound site for about three to four times.

➢ Apply only a mouth suction procedure as a last resort. Rinse your mouth thoroughly with water after spitting out each suctioned envenomed blood. A mouth suction procedure will draw out at least 25% to 30% of the venom.

Skin Diseases

In a survival scenario, the most commonly acquired skin diseases such as boils, fungal infections, and rashes, rarely progress into a severe health issue. However, they distract your focus to survive and cause utter discomfort. You just ought to treat them.

Boils (Furuncles & Carbuncles)

A boil is a sorely painful, pus-filled inflammation circumscribed in certain areas of the skin. Its development begins when bacteria invade to infect and inflame the skin's hair follicles.

TECHNICAL TREATMENT:

✚ **Small Boils (Furuncle)** – The main intent of treating a boil is to destroy the formation of the abscess to relieve the pain. Applying a warm compress over the boil greatly helps to bring it to a head and accelerate pus drainage in the inflamed area.

✚ **Large Boils (Carbuncle)** – Similar to treating smaller boils, compelling to drain pus is the intent of treating carbuncles. However, the treatment requires an invasive procedure by incising the boil.

Use a sterile knife, needle, wire, or similar pointed item to open the boil and drain the pus. Follow up the pus-draining process by applying sterile gauze on the wound to soak up and completely drain extra pus in deeper infections. Cover the boil area and inspect it periodically to ensure no infections develop further.

Fungal Infections

Fungal infections are inflammatory conditions caused by a fungus. They usually occur in your extremities, which are prone to contact fungi and other viral organisms.

TECHNICAL TREATMENT:

✚ Fungi thrive in cool, damp, and wet areas. Therefore, always keep your skin dry and clean. Never scratch the affected area. Instead, expose it to as much sunlight as possible.

Alternative effective treatments require dabbing the affected area with any of these antiseptic substances: chlorine bleach, concentrated salt water, vinegar, alcohol, or tincture of iodine. You may also wash the infected skin with lye soap and running water.

Rashes

Rashes appear as either locally clustered or affecting the entire body. Typically, they are itchy, tiny, reddish, and circular swelling lesions with a central depression on the skin.

They generally build up soon after getting the skin or body into direct contact with an allergen. Chapped dry skin or blisters show up within a day to three days from infection.

Skin or body allergens may include plants, food, drugs, and other infectious agents. Poor hygiene, anxiety, excessive heat exposures, and certain skin diseases like acne and eczema are also common causes of developing rashes.

TECHNICAL TREATMENT:

✚ Hence, to avoid acquiring rashes, it is always noteworthy to identify the specific substances that irritate your skin or the conditions that your skin would react adversely to the instance of contact. In addition, familiarize yourself with the two governing rules for the treatment of rashes:

Rule # 1: If rashes are moist (typical of blisters), then keep them dry.

Never scratch them. Keep weeping rashes dry by using a compress of tannic acid or vinegar or tea obtained from boiling either acorns or bark from a hardwood tree.

Rule # 2: If rashes are dry (typical of chapped dry skin), then keep them moist. Keep dry rashes moistened by rubbing small amounts of grease or rendered animal fat on the affected skin.

As a standard operating procedure, always treat rashes as <u>open wounds</u>. Clean the affected skin daily by either washing with soap and water or using antiseptics. A host of substances is available for survivors in the wild for use as antiseptics to treat wounds (refer to Image-22).

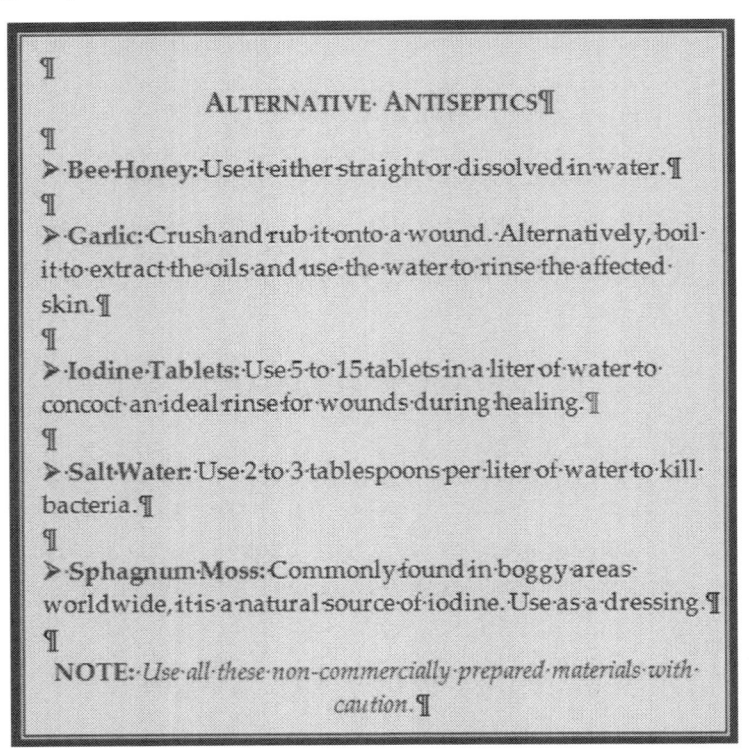

> **ALTERNATIVE ANTISEPTICS**
>
> ➤ **Bee Honey:** Use it either straight or dissolved in water.
>
> ➤ **Garlic:** Crush and rub it onto a wound. Alternatively, boil it to extract the oils and use the water to rinse the affected skin.
>
> ➤ **Iodine Tablets:** Use 5 to 15 tablets in a liter of water to concoct an ideal rinse for wounds during healing.
>
> ➤ **Salt Water:** Use 2 to 3 tablespoons per liter of water to kill bacteria.
>
> ➤ **Sphagnum Moss:** Commonly found in boggy areas worldwide, it is a natural source of iodine. Use as a dressing.
>
> NOTE: *Use all these non-commercially prepared materials with caution.*

Image-22: Alternative Antiseptics Available Around

Environmental Ailments

Distinct from infection or lifestyle diseases, environmental ailments are direct attributions to environmental factors such as extreme exposures to specific temperatures and toxins contained in the air, soil, and water. As a survivor, you could undergo any of these environmental illnesses: frostbite, trench foot, heatstroke, hypothermia, diarrhea, and the acquisition of intestinal parasites.

Frostbite

Frostbite occurs as an injury in frozen tissues or a destruction of the skin and its underlying tissues because of prolonged exposures to freezing or sub-freezing temperatures. Your hands and feet, as well as exposed facial areas like your ears and nose, are particularly prone to frostbite.

The respective tissues in these exposed body areas become immovable and solid. Deep frostbite extends freezing tissues at a depth below the skin. Light frostbite only affects the outer skin surfaces, which can appear in a whitish dull pallor.

While you are with companions, you can prevent frostbite by applying the *'buddy system.'* Inspect often the face of your companions and ensure that they inspect yours. If alone, cover periodically your nose and lower facial areas with your mittens.

TECHNICAL TREATMENT:

✚ Managing frostbite is easy. You simply rub gently the affected area with lukewarm water. Pat the concerned part dry and place it close to your skin, warming it at body temperature.

Never try thawing the affected areas by placing them adjacent to open flames. Subjecting yourself to drastic changes in temperatures can make matters worse.

Trench Foot

A trench foot is a condition that resembles frostbite. It results from prolonged exposure to cold, wet, or damp conditions, at a temperature just above freezing.

In this case, your muscles and nerves sustain more of the damage; however, gangrene may occur. In some extreme cases, the flesh and tissues die, and may consequently necessitate amputation.

TECHNICAL TREATMENT:

✝ Your best prevention from trench foot is keeping your feet dry. Wash daily your feet and ensure its dryness by wearing dry or absorbent socks.

Hyperthermia or Heatstroke

You must maintain a body temperature not exceeding 40.5°C (105°F). Otherwise, your body develops a heatstroke.

Heatstroke is a severe condition caused by an impairment of the temperature-regulating abilities of the body. Oftentimes, it is a result of extended exposures to excessive heat.

Dehydration or cramps, which are usual ailments due to heat, do not typically precede a heatstroke. Its common symptoms characterize a hot dry skin, high fever, severe headache, swollen face, red eyes, and sweating cessation.

In some serious cases, the victim experiences delirium or a temporary state of mental confusion. Thus, anticipate cardiac arrest or conditions of struggling, shouting, shivering, diarrhea, and vomiting from the victim. A heatstroke victim could also collapse and go into a coma or prolonged states of deep unconsciousness.

TECHNICAL TREATMENT:

✤ Find ways to cool the victim as fast as possible. You can dip the victim in a cool stream. Ensure wetting the head. Heat loss over the scalp is a great relief. Provide ample drinking fluids.

If water is scarce, douse the victim with urine. At the very least, apply wet and cold compresses to all the extremities and joints, particularly the armpits, crotch, and neck.

Note by this time that the victim is already in severe shock. During the cooling period, expect a prolonged coma and a heatstroke recurrence within 48 hours.

✤ In cases where the cardiac arrest occurs, prepare to administer CPR. Treat the victim for dehydration with a light mixture of salt and water.

Hypothermia

Hypothermia is the opposite of hyperthermia. When the body's temperature-regulating abilities fail to maintain a normal body temperature of 36°C (97°F) and induce an abnormally low body temperature, hypothermia develops.

Prolonged exposures to cool and cold temperatures are oftentimes the causes of hypothermia. Sometimes, dehydration and deficiencies of rest and food intake predispose a survivor to hypothermia.

Technical Treatment:

✚ Distinct from heatstroke, you must warm gradually the victim of hypothermia. Let the victim wear dry, thick, and warm garments. Replenish lost fluids.

Diarrhea and Dysentery

The inclusive nature of diarrhea as a common and debilitating environmental ailment is due to the shifts in the normal consumptions of food and water sourced from the new survival surroundings. Oftentimes, these alimental sources are unsafe.

Specifically, consuming spoilt food, eating spicy foods, using dirty dishes and utensils, and drinking contaminated water, poor and unsanitary housekeeping cause diarrhea. Several other factors cause diarrhea.

Plain old stress and flu contacted from changing climates can also trigger diarrhea. Traveler's diarrhea, also known as Montezuma's revenge, is a common condition resulting from body fatigue or exhaustion from hiking on long and arduous treks.

Typically, diarrhea is an intestinal disorder characterizing frequent fluid fecal evacuations. These watery stools may be due to bacterial irritations in the alimentary canal and cause recurring abdominal cramps, vomiting, and nausea.

Technically, on one hand, this can develop into a more serious case of invasive diarrhea, also termed as dysentery. It attacks the lower intestinal wall, causing inflammation, ulcers, and abscesses that may lead to the presence of blood and mucus in the stools, high fever, loss of body fluids, and even death.

On the other hand, noninvasive diarrhea bears high risks of dehydration. This condition can also be life-threatening, especially if the victim fails to replenish lost body fluids adequately.

TECHNICAL TREATMENT:

When acquiring diarrhea and you do not have any anti-diarrheal medicines available, either of these following recommended treatments are effective:

✚ Limit your fluid intake for 24 hours. If possible, only drink a cup of a strong tea solution—preferably, concocted from boiling the inner barks of a hardwood tree—every 2 hours until diarrhea stops completely. Tea contains tannic acid that helps to relieve diarrhea.

✚ Make a drink solution containing treated water, dried bones or charcoal, and a handful of ground chalk. If rinds of citrus fruit or some apple pomace are available, add an equal portion to the solution to make it more effective. Take doses of 2 tablespoons of the mixture for every 2 hours until stopping completely diarrhea.

Intestinal Parasites

Intestinal parasites live and feed on other cells in the gastrointestinal tract and walls. To avoid intestinal parasites and worm infestations in the body, the chief preventive measure calls for never going barefoot.

Exposed feet on the ground enable legions of skin-penetrating parasitic species to quickly infest the host body. Their rapid infestations cause loss of appetite, anemia, gastrointestinal distresses, and even death, in some cases.

Further practical remedies demand you not to drink contaminated water and ingest uncooked meat. Be careful also when eating raw vegetables since they may contain traces of human wastes used as fertilizers.

TECHNICAL TREATMENT:

✚ Should you acquire intestinal parasites or worm infestation while lacking the proper medical treatments, you can avail for the maverick home remedies of survivors (refer to Image-23).

HOME REMEDIES FOR INTESTINAL PARASITE INFESTATION

➢ **Hot Peppers:** Peppers are effective, only, if they are steady staples in your diet. You can eat them raw or blend them in soups and meat dishes.

➢ **Kerosene:** Drink no more than 2 tablespoons of kerosene. If necessary, repeat this treatment in a span of 24 to 48 hours. Be careful not to inhale the fumes. They may cause lung irritation.

➢ **Salt Water:** Drink a solution dissolving 4 tablespoons of salt in 1 liter of water. Take this treatment only once.

➢ **Tobacco:** Eat 1 to 1.5 cigarette sticks without the paper and filter. Nicotine in cigarettes kills or stuns the worms long enough for your system to pass them. If the infestations are severe, repeat the treatment in a span of 24 to 48 hours.

NOTE: *These home remedies work on the principle of changing the environment status of the gastro-intestinal tract. Essentially, they create a prohibitive environment to parasitic infestations and attachments.*

Image-23: Unorthodox Home Remedies for Treating Intestinal Parasitic Infestations

Alternative Applications | Herbal Healing

Modern pharmaceutical laboratories, wonder drugs, and equipment have rendered into obscurity those more primitive medical practices involving common sense, practical determination, and a number of simple treatments. However, in several regions of the world, many people still cure their ailments by relying on quackery and alternative medical advice and practices based on experiences and observations in their ignorance of scientific findings.

Many of the plants they use for herbal medications are as effective, if not, more efficient, as the most modern medical treatments available. Fact is that countless modern medications derive their formulations from refined herbs.

Thus, it would be an advantage if you have had prior knowledge of the flora or plant life in certain regions. You shall have to use what is available in any setting.

These settings could also be possible survival scenarios where their plants and vegetation can provide you with the necessary medicines. However, a positive identification of the plants to use for natural remedies is as critical as using them for food.

Equally crucial is the appropriate preparation and usage of these plants. To facilitate you further, learn the following terms used in this manual for the preparation of medicinal herbs and plants for internal or external applications:

- ❖ **Decoction** – Drawing into the water useful chemicals in herbal leaves or other plant parts through boiling and simmering them down. The process uses an average mixing ratio of approximately an ounce to a couple of ounces (28 to 56 grams) of herbs to a half liter of water.

❖ **Expressed Juice** – Denote extracting saps from a plant material and applied directly to the wound or as an ingredient for making another medicine.

❖ **Infusion or Tisane** – Placing a small quantity of an herb in a container filled with hot water, and allowing it to steep prior to direct usage.

❖ **Poultice or Cataplasm** – Crushing herbal leaves or other plant parts. Sometimes, the process requires heating the crushed substances, for which you apply directly to a wound or sore.

The following tables show summaries of applying herbal healing to specific health issues commonly associated with survival scenarios, as well as producing helpful herbal medicines (refer to Image-24A & 24B).

Health Condition	Treatment Application	Herb or Plant Used
Aches Pains Sprains	Treat externally by applying a herbal *poultice* of any of the available herbs	• Chickweed • Dock Or Wood Sorrel • Garlic • Plantain Leaves • Willow Bark
Colds Sore Throats	Treat with a *decoction* or an *infusion* of any of the available herbs	• Burdock Roots • Mallow • Mint Leaves • Mullein Flowers or Roots • Plantain Leaves • Willow Bark
Constipation	Drink a *decoction* of any of the available herbs	• Dandelion Leaves • Rose Hips • Walnut Bark
	Eat raw flowers of	• Daylily
Fevers	Drink an *infusion* of any of the available herbs	• Elder Flowers or Fruit • Linden Flower • Willow Bark
	Drink a *decoction* of	• Elm Bark
Hemorrhoids	Treat with external washes from either tree barks	• Elm • Oak
	Treat with the *expressed juices* of	• Plantain Leaves
	Drink a *decoction* of	• Solomon's Seal Root
Itchiness Plant Rashes Insect Stings Sunburn	Apply a *poultice* of any of the available herbs	• Aloe Vera • Jewelweed Juice • Witch Hazel Leaves

Image-24A

Herbal Medication	Production Process	Herb or Plant Used
Analgesic *for external use only*	Mix the *expressed juices* of any of the herbs available with vegetable oil or animal fat to form a paste or ointment	Chickweed; Dock Or Wood Sorrel; Garlic; Plantain Leaves; Willow Bark
Antihemorrhagic *for external use only*	Create a *poultice* of any of the available herbs	Puffball Mushroom; Plantain Leaves; Yarrow Leaves; Woundwort Leaves
Antifungal Wash *for external use only*	Create a *decoction* of any of the available herbs	Acorns; Oak Bark; Walnut Leaves
Antiseptic *for external use only*	Produce the *expressed juice* from any of the available herbs	Chickweed Leaves; Dock Leaves; Garlic; Wild Onion
	Create a *decoction* of any of the available herbs	Burdock Root; Mallow Leaves; Roots White Oak Bark
Anti-flatulent	Create a *decoction* of either herbs	Carrot Seeds; Mint Leaves
Sedative	Create a *decoction* of any of the available herbs	Mint Leaves; Passionflower Leaves

NOTE: *Many of these herbal remedies work slower than the medicines you know. Therefore, begin with smaller doses. Allow more time for them to take effect.*

WARNING: *These specific natural remedies are for exclusive use only in a survival situation, and not for routine use. Apply herbal medicines with extreme care, and only, when you have limited or deficient medical supplies. Some herbal medicines can be dangerous and cause further damage to your health, or even death.*

Image-24B

"Survival is not so much about the body; but rather, it is about the triumph of the human spirit."

—Danitra Vance, American comedian

STEREOTYPED SURVIVAL SETTINGS & SITUATIONS

"You don't know if you're going to be rescued in a day or a month; prepare for the long haul and make the place your home."

—**Matt Graham**, American TV host, and survivalist

> **DISCLAIMER**
> *The survival tips on this chapter are for informational purposes only. The author takes no responsibility for your actions or usage of the information presented on this manual.*

Prior to leaving your home sweet home, make it a habit to confer this chapter to ensure your safety while away. Its important guidelines will guarantee your preparedness to think prudently and act accordingly to whatever untoward incidents confronting you along the way, regardless of wherever or whenever they happen.

In the event that you will find yourself dealing with a disaster, remember that you should always know what typical environment you are adventuring into—the geographical grounds you will be hiking, the open seas you will be sailing across, the terrain over which you will be flying, or simply, the general nature and assemblage of your destination.

Whatever may be the circumstances—waylaid in the wilds, marooned on an islet, stranded in snow, deserted in a desert, abandoned at sea, coping with manmade/natural calamities in the city—your primordial course of action to take prior to moving along is to apply the Boy Scouts' self-explanatory mnemonic device of *'S.T.O.P.—Stop | Think | Observe | Plan.'*

S.T.O.P. becomes your life-saving principle to maneuver yourself to safety and stay healthy before any help or rescue operations will find you. It becomes your wise weapon to combat and conquer the challenges and complex conditions of the following stereotyped survival scenarios:

Wildish Wildernesses

The wildish wildernesses stand silent witnesses to the countless tales of people getting lost in their territory. Most of these folks found themselves barely alive, as they were not able to apply the necessary skills to stay healthy in spite of nature's bounties in the area.

By nature, these are beautiful environments. It is no wonder why many families spend their time camping each year in the wilderness. However, it is ideal to be prepared and learn the basic survival skills of the jungle or forest before camping out in these wilds.

Jumbled Jungles

The dangers that lie beneath the canopy of evergreen trees making up the jungle are just too numerous to count. The natural environment has been notorious for testing the limits of humans.

A myriad of animal and plant species are present inside the jungle. However, it can be tricky and difficult to tell which of these plant varieties are edible and which are not.

Typical of jungles are their deadly inhabitants such as poisonous snakes and disease-carrying insects. Another particular danger within jungles is the steep levels of wafting bacteria in the atmosphere that could easily sense wounds and injuries to infest within short periods.

Jungles tend to have abundant sources of water. Nevertheless, these water supplies attract bacteria, insects, and other predators. Hence, jungle water usually contains impurities and destructive contaminants.

A commonality in jungle climates is its dampness, humid air, periodic heavy rainfalls, and sudden precipitations. Oftentimes, these weather conditions will leave you inevitably wet and more susceptible to discomforts and illnesses.

Your ability to change clothes or dry those you are wearing is vital. Due to these persistent downpours, seeking and setting up your shelter is necessary during the day. During nighttime though, you will less likely need more warmth.

Fearsome Forests

Similar to jungles, forests are sanctuaries to a cornucopia of flora and fauna. Insects are a dime a dozen in forests, running the gamut of their genetic taxonomy from the irritants to the disease carriers, and to the poisonous ones.

Forests are the kingdoms of both predators and preys. You should learn how to monitor and avoid the tracks of dangerous bears and wildcats, or any other predators native to the region.

When tracking these fierce animals, search the trees and observe the grounds for clues. Broken leaves, bent tips of twigs and branches, slight indentations on the ground that are downright invisible to the normal sight are all enough to dictate where to proceed safely.

You should also be aware that the forest grounds alter constantly while you move along in your path. They hide imminent perils such as large protruding tree roots that may knock you over and deep pits that could trap you.

Tropical forests characterize warm temperatures throughout the year. As it is the case, finding out where your shelter would be or setting it up need not be your top priority during the day. Nonetheless, you will most likely need extra warmth during the later hours.

They also have heavy downpours that maintain their verdant nature of ferns and mosses and growths of luxuriant vegetation. Lest you have some basic knowledge of either fishing or hunting, your food staples will only be limited within the range of edible plants. Of course, you must distinguish them from poisonous plants.

Forests, like jungles, have an abundance of water. Typically, forests grow densely and prosper luxuriantly nearby water sources. However, these water supplies actually imply underground wells, springs, wellsprings, or rainfall instead of streams or rivers.

Tameless Tundra

Alpine tundra is a large ecological expanse located at very high altitudes. The high altitude results in adverse climates, which is too windy and cold.

Its temperature is extremely cold during wintertime while remaining relatively cold during summertime. Occurrences of rainfall are only occasional.

Thus, it is a harsh natural environment where trees cannot grow. Its flora and fauna share common characteristics that only suit the region's specific climatic conditions.

Short grasses, flowering plants, and shrubs only abound in the area. Coyotes, elks, marmots, and an array of insect species populate the alpine tundra.

With decreasing elevation, the alpine tundra transitions to sub-alpine forests below the timberline. With increasing elevation, it peaks on the snow lines where ice persists throughout, even in summer.

Your following S.T.O.P. survival procedures, in order of priority, when you have just discovered yourself waylaid in these wilds (refer to Image-25):

1. Retrace your steps to the last known path.
2. Find a source of drinking water.
3. Create a fire.
4. Find/build a shelter before nightfall.
5. Fashion a weapon you can use for self-defense.
6. Search for food provisions.
7. Wait for rescue operations; travel in one direction during daylight.

Image-25: S.T.O.P. Survival Procedures (Wildish Wilderness)

ISOLATED ISLES

Parallel to those popular cinematic narratives of travelers marooned by a storm or shipwreck, they eventually end up washed ashore on an isolated island. This particular survival scenario presents great opportunities to learn survival techniques and lessons that may also apply in many other settings.

To stay alive, you must learn three basic guidelines for a desert island survival: sourcing out your fresh drinking water and food provisions; constructing your shelter; and, implementing significant SOS signaling and semaphore basics for calling for rescue.

Your following S.T.O.P. survival procedures, in order of priority, when you have just discovered yourself marooned in an isolated islet (refer to Image-26):

1. Find a source of drinking water.
2. Find/build a shelter.
3. Build a fire.
4. Create rescue signals.
5. Search for food provisions.
6. Create tools for catching food.
7. Fashion a weapon you can use for self-defense.
8. Wait for rescue operations; create a raft to leave the island.

Image-26: S.T.O.P. Survival Procedures (Isolated Isle)

Chilling Climates

Surviving in snowy and extremely cold conditions is dangerous due to entailing issues of frostbite and dehydration. Certainly, your biggest priority will be seeking shelter to keep you warm and your body temperature up regularly.

You must also know that finding suitable materials for a winter shelter can be tricky. Therefore, always bear in mind that whenever you spend time outside in the ice and snow, you should never leave home without carrying extra winter clothing— either water-resistant garments or clothing consisting of multiple layers to shield and insulate your body against low temperatures.

If you can start a fire to melt the ice or snow, then water requirements do not really pose a problem in this scenario. However, food will be particularly scarce in an icy or a snowy environment.

During cold climates, insects are unlikely perilous. Yet, it would still be practical and worth checking which species are native or common to the area.

Apart from you, certain creatures also starve under this setting. Bears, wolves, mountain lions, and other winter predators will be seeking actively large and juicy preys—including you.

Your S.T.O.P. survival procedures, in order of priority, when you have just discovered yourself stranded in snow (refer to Image-27):

> 1. Keep yourself warm to avoid hypothermia.
> 2. Find/build a shelter before nightfall.
> 3. Use snow as a source of drinking water.
> 4. Create a fire.
> 5. Search for food provisions.
> 6. Fashion a weapon you can use for self-defense.
> 7. Wait for rescue operations; travel in one direction during daylight. Sleep at night.

Image-27: S.T.O.P. Survival Procedures (Chilling Climate)

Dust Devil Deserts & Dry Domains

Your principal difficulty whenever you find yourself stranded in a desert, with only the shirt on your back, is knowing where to source out water. After all, the availability of water is the most pressing need in surviving in the desert so you can keep your body hydrated while avoiding heat exhaustion and heatstroke.

Lest finding quickly an oasis, water will definitely be scarce, yet, dangerous to obtain. Water procurement in the desert also demands your quick attention to ensuring rations to last your survival.

Similarly, food will be tough to find. Generally, this will require you to have a considerable amount of knowledge on the animal and plant species within the region, as well as their edibility. Yet, no matter how little the signs of life are for seemingly endless miles around, a number of insects and predators is presumptively a cause of concern.

Since dust devil deserts and dry domains characterize exceedingly hot temperatures, it is usual that you easily will drain your energy. Hence, it is also helpful when you know how to conserve your energy; only perform strenuous actions when necessary.

In this case, you will need to keep yourself away from the prickling heat of the sun. As much as possible, avoid direct contact with the naked sun during times you are idle. Therefore, locating and setting up your shelter immediately will be as essential in a desert as it is in a snowy setting.

Nighttime in the desert is infamously cold. This implies that your additional survival task is to gather combustible materials for setting a bonfire to keep you warm while you sleep.

Navigation and orienteering will surely be tough challenges since a desert has only a few to no points of reference or landmarks to base your position or aim for a safer destination. Hence, this will require you to learn how to use the moon, stars, and sun as guides to determine your location.

Your S.T.O.P. survival procedures, in order of priority, when you have just discovered yourself deserted in a desert (refer to Image-28):

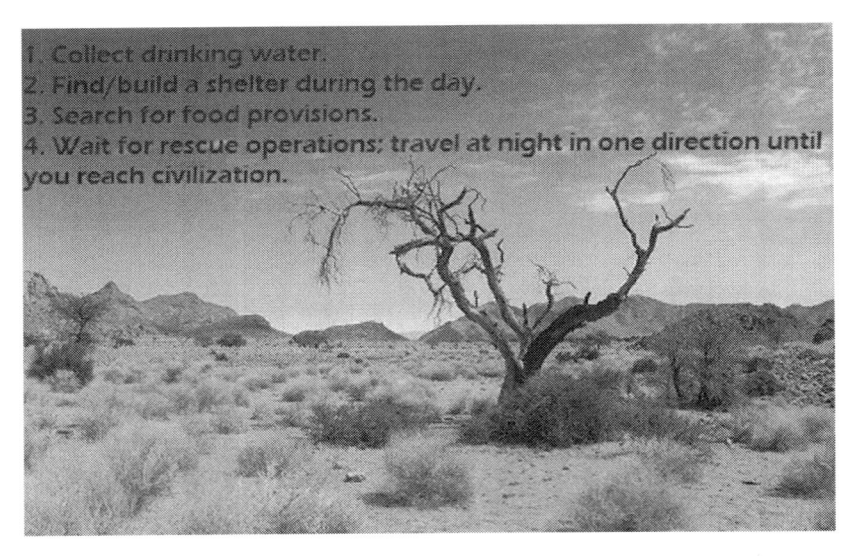

1. Collect drinking water.
2. Find/build a shelter during the day.
3. Search for food provisions.
4. Wait for rescue operations; travel at night in one direction until you reach civilization.

Image-28: S.T.O.P. Survival Procedures (Dust Devil Desert)

OMINOUS OCEANS & CERULEAN COASTS

Just the notion of being completely lost in the open seas is terrifying. It virtually appears that there are no resources in sight, except water, for you to stay alive.

In reality, the ocean has more resources than what you might have initially thought. If all you have everywhere is water and nary a drop to quench your thirst, then compel yourself to make saltwater potable.

Although food could be limited, be grateful for being able to catch and eat raw fish. Just think of it as top-grade sashimi without the wasabi and soy sauce!

An imminent danger when you keep afloat at sea is your direct exposure to the scorching sun, which causes sunburn, dehydration, and heatstroke. In addition, you will have to either avoid the lethal attacks of those usual ocean predators (i.e., orcas or killer whales, sharks, barracudas, stingrays, jellyfish, moray eels, sea anemones, etc.).

However, insects are not as prevalent in the high seas as they are in the land. Oceanic parasites such as sea lice could be bothersome though since they could victimize you with their itchy bites and irritating rashes. Another cause to worry is the flesh-eating sea bug, common in the waters off Australia.

Thus, ensure to build your shelter to protect you from these sea dangers. In most cases, being lost at sea is due to either a sinking boat, plane crash, or a strong undertow that sweeps one out to sea. You can build your shelter or raft from the debris of these mishaps.

Your S.T.O.P. survival procedures, in order of priority, when you have just discovered yourself abandoned at sea:

1. Stay afloat.
2. Find/build shelter during the day.
3. Search for food provisions.
4. Wait for rescue operations; travel at night in one direction until you reach civilization.

Image-28: S.T.O.P. Survival Procedures (Ominous Ocean)

METROPOLIS MISHAPS

Cities are wonderful places to live in and enjoy life, especially when everything is functioning efficiently. Yet, these urban landscapes can be chaotic and devastating environments when there is a complete absence of order, infrastructure, and electricity. If you were living in the city, you would undoubtedly be in more danger.

Fact is that potential urban catastrophes—natural and ecological disasters, urban terrorist attacks, and conventional warfare—can put an entire metropolis in shambles. Such apocalyptic events produce a cataclysmic breakdown in foundational institutions, anarchy or mass civil unrest, and enormous civilian casualties.

Food supply chains, basic service utilities, as well as transport and communication infrastructures would all collapse. If these disastrous effects extend longer than a month's time, a new world order prevails to take place—a dog-eat-dog environment or a retrogression to primitive living.

A proliferation of predators and insects will become part of the major issue. Even your fellow human beings can be your principal threats, especially when you are all competing to seek the same limited resources.

In disaster cases like super typhoons and strong quakes, where they can cause severe damage to urban buildings, you must also be aware to exercise more caution moving in on and around them. These affected structures may be vulnerable to collapse or have already lost their structural integrity. Moreover, watch the grounds as they will have unexpected sinkholes and large cracks. Over time, these structural and geological damages can only worsen.

In a pandemic scenario, water sources, aside from those bottled ones found in convenience stores, will have high possibilities of contamination. You will need to go somewhere else to have access to fresh potable water, food, and energy sources.

You only have two options when any of these crises strike the city: either you stay to protect your home or bug out to live a country life!

Making the right decision could be a dilemma. The bottom line is to ensure that you must have a much safer and better place to go!

Deciding to remain in the city will be a rational choice for many people vis-à-vis their respective reasons and situations. After all, most people depend on the city as their main source of livelihood.

As such, you can always prepare yourself facing all these dire situations. You can continue staying in the ravaged city while living off existing supplies, and thereby, making later preparations for exiting the place at your most appropriate or convenient time.

Upon learning of the implicit dangers, you will subscribe to the belief that the further away and faster you can get yourself out from the populated centers, the better will your chances be for survival. Yet, as you decide otherwise, bugging out towards suburbia will also incur its fair share of troubles and risks.

You may be severely limited as to how much of your valuable things you can carry. Fuel for traveling may only cover a limited range. Besides, you may run the risk of an engine breakdown along your way out.

Exposures to roadblocks, random violence, social chaos, etc. will truly be certainties. Looting incidents will certainly occur in your house while you are away. Worse, you may have nothing left when you get back and everything returns to normalcy.

Your S.T.O.P. survival procedures, in order of priority, when you have just discovered yourself coping with a calamity in the city (refer to Image-30):

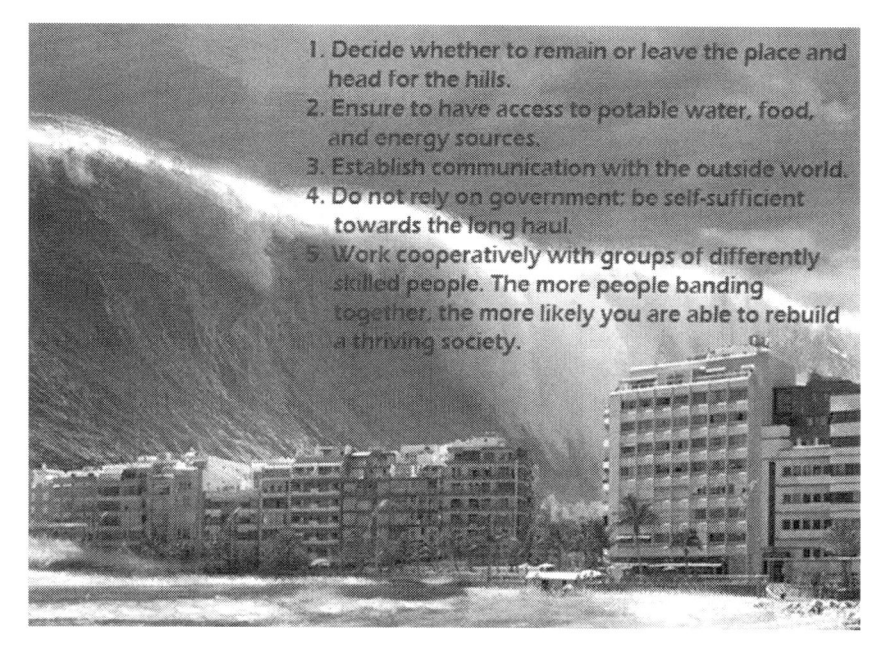

Image-30: S.T.O.P. Survival Procedures (Metropolis Mishap)

1. Decide whether to remain or leave the place and head for the hills.
2. Ensure to have access to potable water, food, and energy sources.
3. Establish communication with the outside world.
4. Do not rely on government; be self-sufficient towards the long haul.
5. Work cooperatively with groups of differently skilled people. The more people banding together, the more likely you are able to rebuild a thriving society.

Manmade Misfortunes & Radioactive Regions

Large-scale or global manmade disasters can be more powerful and fatal than any other known catastrophes. They can actually end the world and wipe out everything in the face of the Earth. In this event, there are practically no survival discussions to talk about nor lessons to learn further.

Yet, some of these small- to medium-scale devastations may occur within a specific or concentrated region. In which case, we can still hope and act to persevere and preserve the sanctity of life.

Technically, you can classify numerous manmade or technological disasters with varying degrees of destruction for both humanity and the environment. The three main types of manmade disasters are biological (i.e., germ warfare using weapons with infectious agents or biological toxins), chemical (i.e., hazardous chemical material spills and other experimental technological accidents), and, nuclear (i.e., radioactive detonation, fallout radiation, and other radiological emergencies).

However, this manual focuses specifically on survival from a nuclear fallout, which incurs relative lethal effects of either a biological or disaster. Thus, they share quite the same survival procedures.

Your primary goal in a nuclear disaster is to mitigate or avoid your exposure to its radioactive particles. Exposures to radioactive fallouts cause radiation poisoning or acute radiation syndrome (ARS)—a collection of health effects occurring within 24 hours of exposure to high levels of radiation.

ARS can damage the DNA and hasten the degeneration of body

cells. Regardless of the severity of radioactive exposure, affected persons will initially experience over-fatigue, vomiting and nausea.

At these earliest signs of trauma or internal contamination, the most recommended treatment application is to take potassium iodide (KI) tablets. A prolonged ARS condition will develop outsets of adverse neurological effects, body deformities, cancer, and even a slow, painful death.

Fallout radiation does not actually remain in suspension in the atmosphere. It decays rapidly at an exponential rate and travels long distances; hence, contaminated areas eventually become relatively safe.

Upon surviving the initial blast, and witnessing the telltale billow of the mushroom-cloud at a distance, exercise the general *'rule of thumb.'* The rule is actually a literal interpretation of stretching your arm out with your thumb raised to the mushroom-cloud.

If you see, (with one of your eyes shut) that the cloud is bigger than your thumb, then it implies that you are within the radiation zone! Thus, you will need to act faster to either evacuate or seek shelter, especially if you are along the direction of the wind from the blast. You only have 10-15 minutes to get somewhere safe.

The further you can go underground, the safer and better. Otherwise, go directly to the center of any high- or low-rise building. Once inside, seal all openings (i.e., windows, doors, and other apertures) and switch off the ventilation systems.

You will also need to remove and discard carefully all your clothing. Clean off thoroughly any radioactive materials that may have settled on your entire body with soap and running water. Else, you will incur *'radiation burns'* on your skin.

After the first 24 hours, the nuclear fallout will have already relinquished about 80% of its total energy; yet, it would still be prudent to stay holed up unless advised otherwise by emergency responders. At this time, you need to prepare for the long haul. Expect to stay put and trapped indoors for a longer time in your shelter, especially when you are located downwind from ground zero.

As such, you will need basic supplies like potable water and food. Ensure to ration carefully whatever provisions you can find.

Listen for news and updates on the emergency radio channels. The government will likely disseminate information on what to do, where to go, what other places you should avoid, or when it is safe to leave your base.

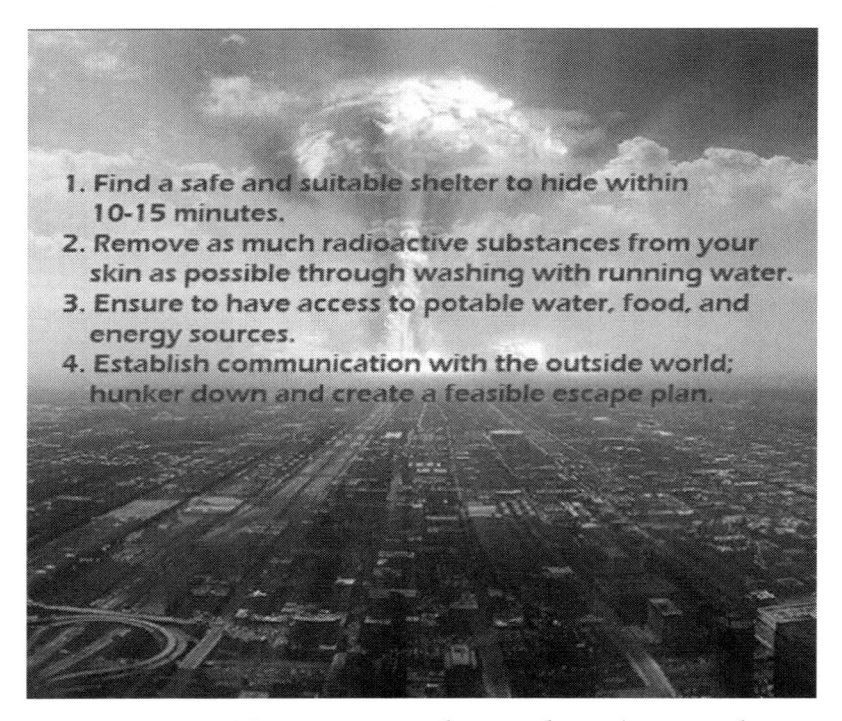

1. Find a safe and suitable shelter to hide within 10-15 minutes.
2. Remove as much radioactive substances from your skin as possible through washing with running water.
3. Ensure to have access to potable water, food, and energy sources.
4. Establish communication with the outside world; hunker down and create a feasible escape plan.

Image-31: S.T.O.P. Survival Procedures (Manmade Misfortunes)

"A survival is a do-or-die situation. The ones who take action, using knowledge and common sense live."

—**Daniel Shrigley**, United States Army veteran

Determining Dangerous Dimensions

"Perhaps, catastrophe is the natural human environment; even though we spend a good deal of energy trying to get away from it, we are programmed for survival amid catastrophes."

—**Germaine Greer**, Australian feminist, public intellectual, and writer

A vital key for surviving in any survival scenario is using whatever available resources within a survival scenario to your favor—whether to use them as medicine, food, materials for making improvised tools or constructing a shelter. The successful application of these available resources depends directly upon your acquired knowledge and absolute or positive identification of each of their nature, characteristics, and qualities.

Knowing poisonous plants, perilous pests, and other ominous obstacles such as wicked waterways and vicious vegetation are as important to a survivor as knowing the safeness and edibility of plants and animals, as well as knowing how to overcome obstacles throughout the survival period. Having a good grasp of all these basic survival knowledge will help you to avoid sustaining illnesses and injuries from them.

Poisonous Plants

Plant poisoning covers a range of ill effects, from a minor irritation to a serious consequence such as death. Typically, plants can poison humans via ingestion, direct contact, and inhalation or absorption.

However, it would be difficult to determine the toxicity or how severely poisonous a plant is because of a variety of reasons. For one, the level of resistance to plant toxicities varies with each individual. Another, every plant has varying contents of toxins due to variations in subspecies and growing conditions.

Several poisonous plants resemble their edible relatives or appear to be like other edible plants. Some can only be edible during specific seasons of the year or at certain stages of their growth.

Moreover, some plants have parts that are either edible or poisonous. Some plants become edible after preparing them using a specific method, but poisonous when raw. Others become toxic after they wilt.

The bottom line is that no unitary rules identify poisonous plants. However, there are certain rules for avoiding poisonous plants (refer to Image-32).

> **BASIC GUIDELINES IN AVOIDING POTENTIALLY POISONOUS PLANTS**
>
> You must stay away from any wild or unknown plants that possess the following:
>
> - Almond scent in its leaves and woody parts
> - Beans, bulbs, or seeds inside pods
> - Bitter or soapy taste
> - Dill-, carrot-, parsnip-, or parsley-like foliage
> - Grain heads with pink, purple, or black spurs
> - Milky or discolored sap
> - Spines, fine hairs, or thorns
> - Three-leaved growth pattern
>
> **NOTE:** *Never eat mushrooms in a survival situation! Offer no room for any experimentation for its edibility because mushroom identification is very difficult in the first place.*
>
> *Typically, mushroom poisoning affects the gastrointestinal and central nervous systems. Some mushrooms have no known antidote. Others cause a quick death.*
>
> *Avoid coming in contact with or touching plants unnecessarily.*

Image-32: Basic Guidelines in Avoiding Potentially Poisonous Plants

Your best policy, therefore, is to acquire the knowledge and ability to identify a plant, with absolute certainty, about its applications or dangers. However, this may not be possible in many instances.

Alternatively, if you own little to no knowledge about the local flora in those expected areas, confer with the following guidelines (refer to Image-33):

UNIVERSAL PLANT EDIBILITY TEST

1. Cut and separate the potential food plant into its basic components—leaves, roots, stems, buds, and flowers. Test only one part of the food plant at a time.
2. Before beginning the edibility test, abstain from any food intake for 8 hours. Throughout the test period, you must only take in purified water and the plant specimen.
3. During the 8-hour abstention period, test the specimen for contact poisoning. Place the specimen on the inner side of your elbow or wrist. Allow a maximum of 15 minutes for observing any reactions (i.e., burning, stinging, itching, numbing, or other irritation); if no reaction occurs, proceed with the test.
4. Select a small portion of the specimen and prepare it the way you plan to eat it.
5. Before eating the prepared specimen, let the outer surface of your lip touch a small portion of it. Allow a maximum of 3 minutes for observing any reactions; if no reaction occurs, proceed with the test.
6. Place the prepared specimen on your tongue. Allow a maximum of 15 minutes for observing any reactions; if no reaction occurs, proceed with the test.
7. Chew thoroughly a pinch of the prepared specimen and hold it in your mouth. DO NOT SWALLOW. Allow a maximum of 15 minutes for observing any reactions; if no reaction occurs, proceed with the test.
8. Swallow the prepared specimen. Wait for 8 hours for a reaction to occur. If any ill effects occur, induce vomiting and drink plenty of water; discontinue with the test. If no reactions occur, eat ¼ cup of the same plant prepared the same way. Wait for another 8 hours. If no reactions occur, then the plant part, as prepared, is safe for eating.

NOTE: *Each part of a plant requires an edibility-testing period of more than 24 hours. Therefore, ensure that there is a sufficient supply of the plant variety to make the testing worth your time and effort.*

Image-33: Universal Plant Edibility Test

As much as possible, learn about the plant life of the areas where you expect to be traveling or working. More importantly, learn to identify and use these plants appropriately in a survival scenario.

To facilitate your learning, avail helpful plant information sources such as books, botanical gardens, films, local markets, natives in the area, nature trails, and pamphlets. Collate and cross-reference data from as many these sources as you can since most of them will not contain all your needed information.

Perilous Pests

Animals rarely are as menacing to the survivor as most of the elements of the environment. Common sense dictates the survivor to avoid confrontations with bears, lions, and other dangerous animals. It further tells you to stay clear of large and heavy grazing animals with hooves and horns.

Your cautious actions will prevent unexpected animal encounters. Be vigilant moving through their environment. Never attract large predators by leaving or scattering food around your shelter site. Survey the scenario carefully prior to entering forests or fording waterways.

Year after year, a number of people figure in dangerous encounters and accidents with various perilous pests (i.e., attacked by bears, mauled by alligators, and bitten by sharks). Most of these incidents though were in some way the fault of the victim.

However, in most circumstances, smaller animals actually exist to be more of a threat to the survivor compared to large animals. To compensate for their diminutive size, nature has bestowed upon several of them distinctly potent weapons such as stingers and fangs to defend themselves.

Each year more victims die from bites by relatively small yet venomous snakes than by large dangerous animals. More victims even die from allergic reactions to bee stings.

For this reason, this manual focuses more attention to smaller yet potentially more dangerous creatures you are more likely to meet as you trespass unwittingly into their habitat; or conversely, these pests slip unnoticed into your environment.

Keeping a level head and an awareness of your surroundings will keep you alive if you use a few simple safety procedures. Do not let curiosity and carelessness kill or injure you.

WICKED WATERWAYS

In a survival situation, you may have to cross a water obstacle. It may be in the form of a river, stream, lake, bog, quicksand, quagmire, or muskeg. Even in the desert, flash floods occur, making streams an obstacle. You must know how to cross them safely.

Rivers | Streams | Channels | Canals

Develop a good plan prior to crossing a river. Your primary step is to find an elevated spot; or, climb a tree where you can obtain a panoramic view of the waterway. From your position, you can distinguish feasible and safe location to cross, as well as to avoid areas that pose potential hazards (refer to Image 34).

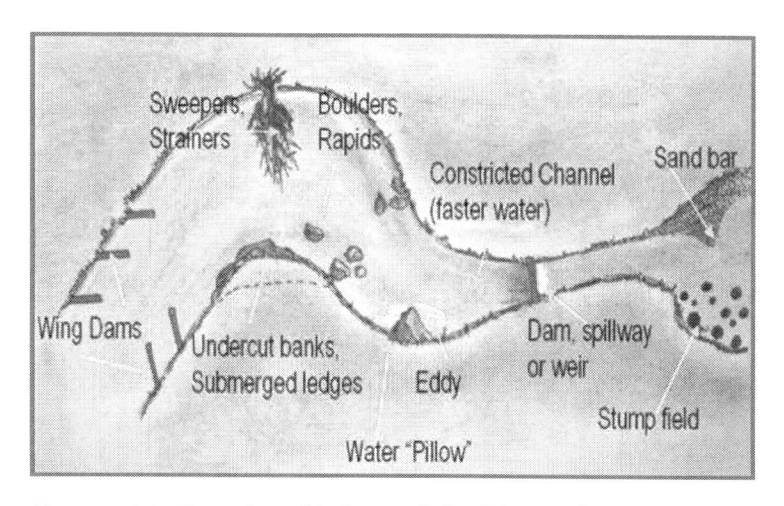

Image-34: Overhead View of the Typical River Risks

These waterways may be narrow or wide, slow or fast moving, and shallow or deep. However, the depth of a crossable river or stream is not a deterrent if you can only keep your footing.

Fact is that deep waterways sometimes flow more slowly, and as such, safer as opposed to shallow fast-moving waterways like rapids. For your general guide in crossing rivers, confer with Image-35.

SUGGESTED SAFE SITES IN CROSSING WATERWAYS

- ❖ A level stretch where it breaks into several channels – Two or three narrow channels are usually easier to cross than a wide river.
- ❖ A sandbar or shallow bank – If possible, select a point upstream from the bank or sandbar so that the current will carry you to it if you lose your footing.
- ❖ A course across the river that leads downstream – so that you will cross the current at about a 45° angle

POTENTIAL PERILS POSED IN CROSSING WATERWAYS

- ❖ Deep or Rapid Waterfall | Deep Channel – Never try to ford a stream directly above or even close to such hazards.
- ❖ Eddies – An eddy can produce a powerful backward pull downstream of the obstruction causing the eddy and pull you under the surface.
- ❖ Estuary – An estuary is normally wide, has strong currents, and is subject to tides. These tides can influence some rivers many kilometers from their mouths. Go back upstream to an easier crossing site.
- ❖ Ledge of Rocks Crossing the River – This often indicates dangerous rapids or canyons.
- ❖ Obstacles on the Opposite Bank that Hinder further Travel – Try to select the spot from which travel will be the safest and easiest.
- ❖ Rocky Places – You may sustain serious injuries from slipping or falling on rocks. Usually, submerged rocks are very slick, making balance extremely difficult. An occasional rock that breaks the current, however, may help you.

Image-35: Summary Guidelines for Crossing a River

Never attempt to wade or swim across a waterway when its waters have extremely low temperatures. Crossing the waters under exceedingly cold conditions could be fatal. Instead, try to build a raft. You can only wade across if the water's depth ensures wetting only your feet. Dry your feet immediately once reaching the bank across.

Rapids

Typically, rapids are either shallow or deep portions of a river that possess extremely fast-moving currents. Generally, the steep descents in the riverbed cause the rapidity of the water flow.

For swimming across the rapids safely, the basic rule is to swim along with the current and never against it. Ensure keeping your body horizontal to the water lest the water current will pull you under.

In shallow rapids, lie on your back, feet pointing downstream, finning your hands alongside your hips. This action will increase buoyancy and help you steer away from obstacles. Keep your feet up to avoid getting them bruised or caught by rocks.

In deep rapids, lie on your belly, with your head downstream and angling toward the shore. Watch for obstacles and be careful of backwater eddies and converging currents, as they often contain dangerous swirls. Converging currents occur where new watercourses enter the river or large obstacles (i.e., islets or boulders, protruding rocks, spillways, etc.) divert around the flow.

As a summary, apply the following steps whenever you cross a swift and treacherous stream like rapids (refer to Image-36A, 36B & 36C).

CROSSING SOLO ACROSS THE RAPIDS

❖ Remove your outer garments to reduce the water's pull on you. Keep your footwear on to protect your feet and ankles from rocks; this will also provide you with a firmer footing.

❖ If you have no pack, tie your pants and other articles in a bundle or to the top of your rucksack. In this manner, if you have to let go of them, all these items will be together. It is easier to find one large pack than to find several small items.

❖ Carry your pack well up on your shoulders and be sure you can easily remove it, if necessary. Not being able to let release a pack quickly enough can drag even the strongest swimmers down.

❖ Find a strong pole about 3 inches (7.5 cm.) in diameter and 8 feet (2.4 m) long to help you ford the stream. Grasp the pole and plant it firmly on your upstream side to break the current.

❖ Plant your feet firmly with each step, and move the pole forward a little downstream from its previous position, but still upstream from you.

❖ With your next step, place your foot below the pole. Keep the pole well slanted so that the force of the current keeps the pole against your shoulder, as shown:

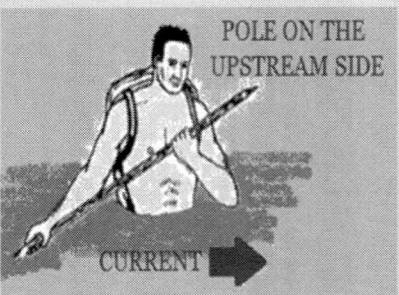

❖ Cross the stream so that you will cross the downstream current at a 45-degree angle. Using this method, you can safely cross water currents that are usually too strong for a person to stand against.

Image-36A: Summary Guidelines for Crossing a River Rapid (Alone)

CROSSING ACROSS THE RAPIDS WITH COMPANIONS (POLE)

If you have companions, cross the stream together. Let your companions prepare his or her pack and clothing the way you prepare yours when crossing solo.

Position the lightest person on the upstream end of the pole and the heaviest on the downstream end. By this method, the upstream person breaks the current to form an eddy, and thus, enabling those below to move with relative ease in the eddy.

If the upstream person stumbles or loses balance temporarily, the others can hold steadily on the pole while he regains his footing, as shown.

Lighest Person in Upstream Position   **Heaviest Person in Downstrean Position, Acting as Anchor**

POLE PARALLEL TO CURRENT ⇨

Image-36B: Summary Guidelines for Crossing a River Rapid (with Company Using a Pole)

CROSSING ACROSS THE RAPIDS WITH COMPANIONS (ROPE)

For three or more people crossing the rapids, procure a sturdy rope, which must be approximately thrice the width of the stream. Perform the crossing technique, as shown.

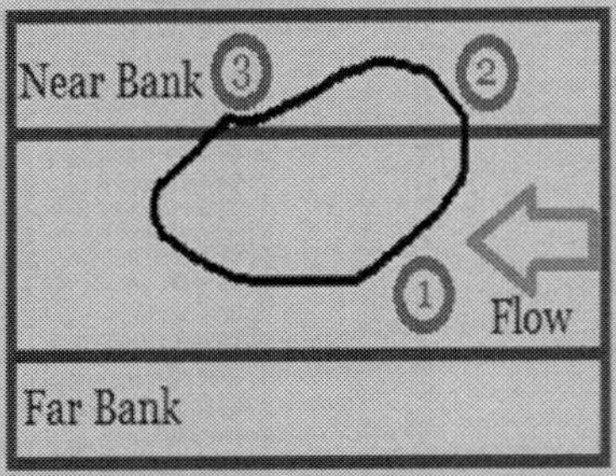

#1 is the strongest person, who secures his chest to the loop, will cross first. #2 & #3, both untied, slacken the rope as necessary and at the same time, enable to stop #1 from being washed away.

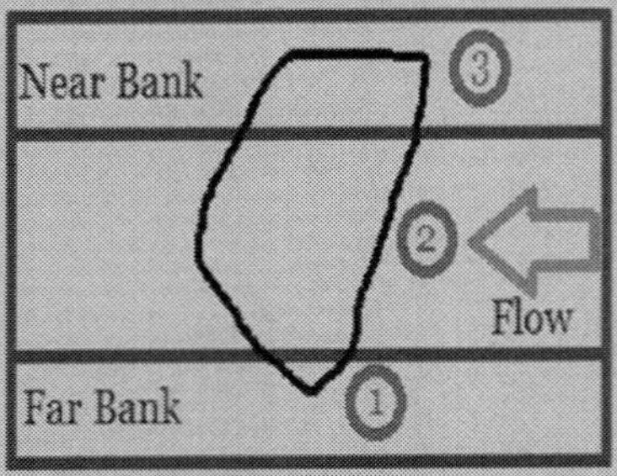

#1 unties himself from the loop after reaching the far bank. #2 ties on and crosses. The others control the rope. Any number of people can be delivered across in this manner.

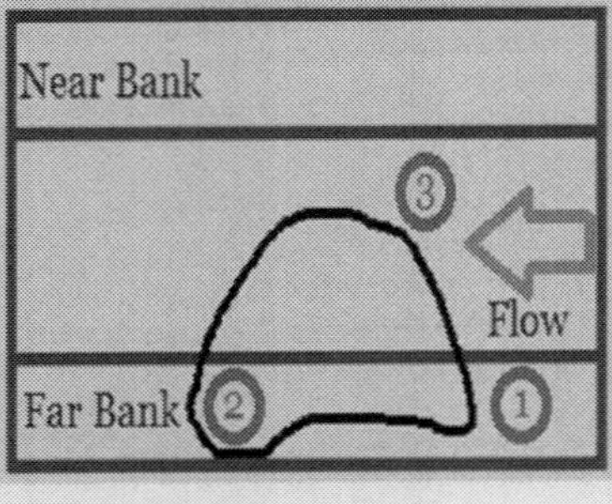

When #2 reaches the far bank, #3 ties on and crosses. #1 will be taking most of the strain to control the rope; but, #2 will be ready in case anything goes wrong.

Image-36C: Summary Guidelines for Crossing a River Rapid (with Company Using a Rope)

Other Waterway Obstacles

Other water obstacles that you may face are bogs, muskeg, quagmire, or quicksand. Do not try to walk across these. Trying to lift your feet while standing upright will make you sink deeper. Try to bypass these obstacles. If you are unable to bypass them, you may be able to span a bridge using logs, branches, or foliage.

A way to cross a bog or muskeg is to lie face down, with your arms and legs spread. Use a flotation device or form pockets of air in your clothing. Swim or pull your way across moving slowly and trying to keep your body horizontal.

In swamps, the areas that have vegetation are usually firm enough to support your weight. However, vegetation will usually not be present in open mud or water areas. If you are an average swimmer, however, you should have no problem swimming, crawling, or pulling your way through miles of bog or swamp.

Quicksand is a mixture of water and sand that forms a shifting mass with varying depths. It yields easily to pressure that it sucks down and engulfs objects resting on its surface.

Quicksand occurs commonly near the mouths of large rivers, in silt-choked rivers with shifting watercourses, and on flat shores. If you are uncertain whether a sandy area is a quicksand, toss a small stone on it. The stone will sink in quicksand.

Although quicksand has more suction than muck or mud, you can cross it just as you would cross a bog. Lie face down, spread your arms and legs, and move slowly across.

Vicious Vegetation

Some water areas you must cross may have underwater and floating plants that will make swimming difficult. However, you can swim through relatively dense vegetation if you remain calm and do not thrash about.

Stay as near the surface as possible and use the breaststroke with shallow leg and arm motion. Remove the plants around you as you would with your clothing. When you get tired, float or swim on your back until you have rested enough to continue with the breaststroke.

The mangrove swamp is another type of obstacle that occurs along tropical coastlines. Mangrove trees or shrubs throw out many prop roots that form dense masses. To get through a mangrove swamp, wait for low tide.

If you are on the inland side, look for a narrow grove of trees and work your way seaward through these. You can also try to find the bed of a waterway or creek through the trees and follow it to the sea.

If you are on the seaward side, work inland along streams or channels. Be on the lookout for crocodiles that you find along channels and in shallow water. If there are any near you, leave the water and scramble over the mangrove roots.

While crossing a mangrove swamp, it is possible to gather food from tidal pools or tree roots. To cross a large swampy vegetation area, construct some type of raft.

"Extinction is the rule. Survival is the exception."

—**Carl Sagan**, American cosmologist, astronomer, astrobiologist, and astrophysicist

Five Fundamental Survival Skills

"The more survival skills an individual has that have been practiced physically and otherwise, the better odds they have for those skills coming to the forefront during a stressful emergency."

—**Cody Lundin**, American survival instructor

Wherever you are planning to go, especially for an extended period, it is always wise to have learned and practiced a survival skill or two. You will never know when you will need it and how important it may preserve the life of others…and yours!

There are many different survival products available in the market, yet they are generally for convenience. The truth of the matter is that, with clever thinking, common sense, and ingenuity, you can actually sustain yourself—even for the long run—by using only the limited resources available or what nature provides in your survival scenario.

All you ever need to survive in whatever survival scenario that fate thrusts you into is some solid foundational survival knowledge. The psychological preparations, facilitation of emergencies thru first aid, and the rest of the survival lessons learned before reaching this chapter are as equally important and essential as the following fundamental survival skills, which you must know like the palm of your hand:

SURVIVAL SKILL # 1: SECURING SHELTER

Whenever forced into survival scenarios, you will certainly get into serious trouble due to direct exposure to the harsh elements of nature. Securing your shelter will directly resolve this burdensome issue.

Foremost, a shelter can protect you from either exceedingly hot or cold temperatures, a host of insects, rain, wind, snow, and the piercing heat of the sun. It can provide you quickly with a sense of well-being and security. As such, it can be your anchor to keep your will to survive.

In some circumstances or environmental areas, your need for shelter may take precedence over your need for food; and possibly, even your need for water. For instance, a prolonged exposure to a cold climate can cause excessive fatigue and weakness (exhaustion). Hence, an exhausted individual can develop a passive outlook, and thereby, lose the will to survive.

The most common error in making a shelter is to make it too large. A shelter must be large enough to protect you. It must also be small enough to contain your body heat, especially in cold climates.

Hereunder are some factors to consider when you plan to build your survival shelter:

- **Group or Personal Shelter**

- **Heat Source** (fire-heated or body-heated)

- **Insulation** (from air, wind, rain or ground)

- **Location** (away from hazards, near materials)

Site Selection

When you are in a survival scenario and realize it is a high priority to set up your shelter, begin looking for a suitable site as soon as possible. While doing so, bear in mind what your requirements are at the site. Two basic requisites are:

❖ It must consist of materials to construct the type of shelter you need.

❖ It must be level enough and large enough for you to move and lie down comfortably.

In some areas, the temperature or season of the year has a strong influence on the site you select. Ideal shelter sites differ in winter and summer. When thinking about your shelter site selection, apply the keyword *B.L.I.S.S.* as your guide:

B - Blend in with the surroundings

L - Low silhouette roofing

I - Irregular shape

S - Secluded location

S - Small

You must also keep in mind the common issues that may arise in your survival environment:

❖ Avoid areas near bodies of water that are below the highest watermark line.

❖ Avoid flash flood areas in foothills.

❖ Avoid rockslide or avalanche areas in mountainous terrain.

Shelter Styles

There are numerous types of shelters to consider such as naturally built shelters (i.e., hollow stumps and logs, caves, etc.), as well as building shelters such as a tree-pit snow shelter, debris hut, lean-to, swamp bed, beach shade, and desert or underground shelters. However, the type of shelter or protection you need depends on your survival scenario. You must also consider asking yourself the following:

❖ How much of my time and effort will I need to build my planned shelter?

❖ Would my proposed shelter protect myself adequately from the elements (i.e., snow, rain, wind, sun, etc.)?

❖ Do I have the tools to build it? Can I make improvised tools?

❖ Do I have the particular type of materials or sufficient resources needed to build it?

To help you answer these questions, you will need to know how to build various types of survival shelters:

> **TREE-PIT SNOW SHELTER**
>
> **Materials/Resources:**
> - A tree with bushy branches to provide overhead cover
> - Evergreen boughs
>
> **Construction Procedure:**
> 1. Dig the snow out around the tree trunk until you reach the diameter and depth you desire, or until you reach the ground.
> 2. Pack the snow around the top and the inside of the hole to provide support.
> 3. Place the evergreen boughs over the top of the pit to give you additional overhead cover. Place evergreen boughs in the bottom of the pit for insulation.

Image-37: Tree-Pit Snow Shelter Description

BASIC LEAN-TO SHELTER

Materials/Resources:

- Any available material for covering such as a poncho or a parachute canvas
- A rope or parachute suspension line, 2-3 meters long
- 3-stakes, about 30-cm. long
- 2-upright poles, or find two trees 2-3 meters apart

Construction Procedure:

1. Before selecting the trees you will use or the location of your poles, check the wind direction. Ensure that the back of your lean-to will be into the wind.
2. Tie off the hood of the poncho. Pull the drawstring tight, roll the hood lengthwise, fold it into thirds, and tie it off with the drawstring.
3. Cut the rope in half. On one long side of the poncho, tie half of the rope to the corner grommet. Tie the other half to the other corner grommet.
4. Attach a drip stick (about a 10-centimeter stick) to each rope about 2.5 centimeters from the grommet. These drip sticks will keep rainwater from running down the ropes into the lean-to. Tying strings (about 10 centimeters long) to each grommet along the poncho's top edge will allow the water to run to and down the line without dripping into the shelter.
5. Tie the ropes about waist high on the trees (uprights). Use a round turn and two half hitches with a quick-release knot.
6. Spread the poncho and anchor it to the ground, putting sharpened sticks through the grommets and into the ground.

NOTE: *If you are expecting a downpour, or planning to use this shelter for more than one night, build a center support for the lean-to. Make this support with a line. Attach one end of the line to an overhanging branch and the other end to the poncho hood. Ensure no slack in the line. Alternatively, you can put an upright stick under the center of the lean-to. However, this method will be restricting your movements and space in the shelter.*

For extra protection from rain or wind, place your rucksack, some brush, or other equipment at the sides of the lean-to. Note that when you are at rest, you lose as much as 80% of your body heat to the ground. To reduce heat loss to the ground, place some type of insulating material, such as pine needles or leaves, inside your lean-to.

Image-37

FIELD-EXPEDIENT LEAN-TO

Materials/Resources:

- 2-upright poles, or find two trees 2-3 meters apart
- 1-pole, 2.5 cm. diameter × 2 meters long
- 5 to 8 poles (for beams), 2.5 cm. diameter × 3 meters long
- Cord or vines for securing the horizontal support to the trees
- Other poles, saplings, or vines for crisscrossing the beams

Construction Procedure:

1. Tie the 2-meter pole to the two trees at waist to chest height. This is the horizontal support. If a standing tree is not available, construct a biped using Y-shaped sticks or two tripods.
2. Place one end of the beams (3-meter poles) on one side of the horizontal support. As with all lean-to type shelters, be sure to place the lean-to's backside into the wind.
3. Crisscross saplings or vines on the beams.
4. Cover the framework with brush, leaves, pine needles, or grass, starting at the bottom and working your way up like shingling.
5. Place straw, leaves, pine needles, or grass inside the shelter for bedding.

NOTE: *During cold weather, add comfort to your lean-to by building a fire reflector wall. Drive 4-1.5-meter long stakes into the ground to support the wall. Stack green logs on top of one another between the support stakes. Form two rows of stacked logs to create an inner space within the wall that you can fill with dirt. This action not only strengthens the wall but also, makes it more heat-reflective. Bind the top of the support stakes so that the green logs and dirt will stay in place.*

With only a little extra effort, you can provide a drying rack. Cut a few 2-cm diameter poles (length depends on the distance between the horizontal support of the lean-to's and the top of the fire reflector wall). Lay one end of the poles on top of the reflector wall and the other end to the lean-to support. Place smaller sticks across these poles and tie them in place; you will now have a place to dry meat or fish and clothes.

Image-38

Debris Hut

Materials/Resources:

- 2-short stakes
- 1-long ridgepole
- A bunch of large sticks, finer sticks, brush, and insulating materials (i.e., grass, pine needles, leaves)

Construction Procedure:

1. Use two short stakes and a long ridgepole to make a tripod by placing one end of a long ridgepole on top of a sturdy base.
2. Secure firmly the ridgepole (pole running the length of the shelter) by anchoring it to a tree at about your waist's height.
3. Prop large sticks along both sides of the ridgepole to create a wedge-shaped ribbing effect. Ensure the ribbing is wide enough to accommodate your body and steep enough to shed moisture.
4. Place finer sticks and brush crosswise on the ribbing. These form a latticework that will keep the insulating materials from falling through the ribbing into the sleeping area.
5. If possible, add light and dry soft debris over the ribbing until the insulating material is at least 1-meter thick or more.
6. Place a 30-cm. layer of insulating material inside the shelter.
7. At the entrance, pile insulating materials that you can drag to you once inside the shelter to close the entrance.
8. Add branches or shingling materials on top of the debris layer to prevent the insulating material from blowing away during a storm.

Image-40: Debris Hut Description

The Lost Ways

SWAMP BED

Materials/Resources:

- 4-trees clustered in a rectangle, or cut four poles (preferably, bamboo)

Construction Procedure:

1. Drive each pole into the ground firmly so that they form a rectangle. They should be far enough apart and sturdy enough to support your weight and height, including equipment.
2. Cut two poles that span the width of the rectangle. They, too, must be strong enough to support your weight.
3. Secure these two poles to the trees (or poles). Be sure they are high enough above the ground or water to allow for tides and high water.
4. Cut additional poles that span the rectangle's length. Lay them across the two side poles, and secure them. (You may use a rope and fashion out a lattice work for the bed frame as a replacement of cut poles)
5. Cover the top of the bed frame with broad leaves or grass to form a soft sleeping surface.
6. Build a fire pad by laying clay, silt, or mud on one corner of the swamp bed and allow it to dry.

Image-41: Swamp Bed Description

Desert Shelters

Materials/Resources:

If you have available materials such as a parachute canvas or poncho, use it along with the desert terrain features such as mounds of sand, rock outcropping, or a depression between rocks or dunes to build your shelter.

Construction Procedure:

In Rocky Sites:

1. Anchor one end of your material, say, poncho on the edge of the outcrop. Fasten it by using rocks or other heavy objects as weights, and lay them on top the edges.
2. Extend the other end of the poncho and anchor it on top of another edge of an outcrop so that it provides the best possible shade.

In Sandy Sites:

1. Pile mounds of sand or use the side of a sand dune as one side of the shelter.
2. Anchor one end of your available material on top of the mound. Fasten it by using sand or other heavy objects as weights, and lay them on top the edges.
3. Extend the other end of the material and anchor it on top of the other mound of sand so that it provides the best possible shade.

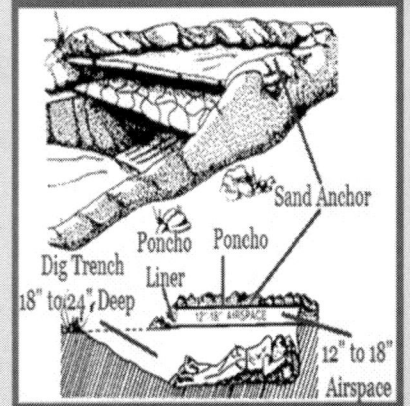

NOTE: *If you have more of the available material, fold it in half and form a 12" to 24" (30-cm. to 45-cm.) airspace between the two halves. This airspace will reduce the temperature under the shelter. In an arid environment, consider the time, effort, and material needed to make your shelter.*

Image-42: Desert Shelter Description

The Lost Ways

Beach Shade Shelter

Materials/Resources:

- Find and collect natural materials like driftwood (for support beams and as a digging tool).
- Gather other natural materials like grass or leaves (for beddings)

Construction Procedure:

1. Select a location that is above the highest water line mark.
2. Dig out a trench running north to south so that it receives the least amount of sunlight. Build the trench wide and long enough for you to move and lie down comfortably.
3. Pile mounds of soil on the three sides of the trench. The higher your pile is, the more space you will have inside the shelter.
4. Lay the support beams spanning the trench on top of the mound; this will form the framework for your roof.
5. Spread and pile up leaves and grasses on the floor to form and serve as your bed.

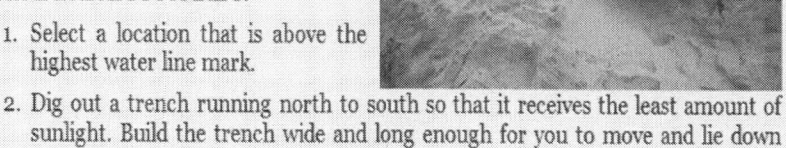

Image-43: Beach Shade Shelter Description

David Kennedy

Natural Shelters

Natural formations can provide shelter. Examples are caves, rocky crevices, clumps of bushes, small depressions, large rocks on leeward sides of hills, large trees with low-hanging limbs, and fallen trees with thick branches. However, when selecting a natural formation, note the following:

❖ *Stay away from low ground such as ravines, narrow valleys, or creek beds. Low areas collect the heavy cold air at night and are therefore colder than the surrounding high ground. Thick, brushy, low ground also harbors more insects.*

❖ *Check for poisonous snakes, ticks, mites, scorpions, and stinging ants.*

❖ *Look for loose rocks, dead limbs, coconuts, or other natural growth that could be your shelter.*

Image-44: Beach Shade Shelter Description

SURVIVAL SKILL # 2: WATER WHEREWITHAL

Among your most urgent needs is water. Without water, you cannot survive longer, especially in hot environments where you lose greater quantities of body fluids rapidly through excessive perspiration. Even in cold areas, you require at least 2 liters of water daily to maintain efficiency.

More than 75% of your body is composed of fluids. To review, your body loses fluid due to exertion, stress, heat, and cold. In order for your body to function effectively, you must replace your lost body fluids. Therefore, one of your primary goals in a survival mode is obtaining an adequate water supply.

Safe Supply Sources

Bottled water is your safest and best bet for your water requirements. However, if it is not available, especially midst a natural or manmade calamity in the city, you will need to obtain it from taps drawing from covered reservoirs, water tanks, or deep wells. A suburban home or a farm has the ideal types of wells.

Nonetheless, wherever you may be, almost all survival environments have water present to a certain extent (refer to Image 45A, 45B & 45C).

Area	Water Source	Procurement Method	Remarks
Sea	Sea	Use a desalting kit	Never drink saltwater without desalting
	Sea Ice		Opaque or grayish sea ice is salty. Crystalline or bluish sea ice contains only little salt. Never use it without desalting.
Beach	Rain	Catch rain in a water-holding material or containers	If the holding material has encrusted salt, wash it in the sea before using.
	Ground	Dig a hole in the ground, deep enough to allow water to seep in. Obtain rocks, build fire, and heat the rocks in water; hold a cloth over the hole to absorb steam. Wring the water from cloth.	If a container or a bark pot is available: Fill the container with seawater; build fire and boil water to produce steam; hold cloth over container to absorb steam; wring the water from cloth.
Frigid Sites	Snow Ice	Melt and purify	Never consume without melting. Snow and ice are no purer than the water from which they come. Consuming snow and ice can reduce body temperature and leads to dehydration.
Desert	Cacti	Cut off the top of a barrel cactus. Mash or squeeze the pulp. Never eat the pulp. Instead, place it in your mouth; suck out its juice and discard it.	Cutting into a cactus is difficult without a machete. Besides, it takes you time since you must get past its long and sturdy spines before cutting through the tough rind.
	Ground (porous rocks, rock outcrops, fissures, and oasis)	In rock fissures, insert flexible tubing and siphon off water.	Also found in valleys, foot of cliffs, concave banks of dry river beds, sunken area behind first sand dune of dried lakes, damp sand

Image-45A: List of Water Sources in Various Environments

Water Supply Indicator (Trees)	Procurement Method
Banana Plantain	Cut down the tree, leaving a stump of about a foot (30-cm.), and scoop out the center of the stump so that the hollow is bowl-shaped. Water from the roots will immediately start to fill the hollow. The first three fillings of water will be bitter, but succeeding fillings will be palatable. The stump will supply water for up to four days. Ensure to cover the stump after to prevent infestation of insects.
Palm, Coconut, Buri, Rattan, Sugar, and Nipa	Bruise a lower frond and pull it down so the tree will bleed at the injury. Milk from green (unripe) coconuts is a good thirst quencher. However, milk from mature coconuts contains oil that acts as a laxative. Drink in moderation only.
Traveler's Tree	A native to Madagascar, this tree has a cuplike sheath at the base of its leaves in which water collects.
Umbrella Tree	Prevalent in the western tropics of Africa, its roots and leaf bases can provide water.
Baobab Tree	Common in Africa and the sandy plains of northern Australia, it collects water in its bottlelike trunk during the wet season. Oftentimes, you can find clear and fresh water in these trees after several weeks of dry weather.
Green Bamboo Thickets	Water from green bamboo is odorless and clear. To obtain the water, bend a green bamboo stalk; tie it down, and then, cut off the top. The water will drip freely during the night. Old, cracked bamboo may also contain water.

Image-45B

Ants or bees going into some hole in a tree also indicate the presence of water. You only need to siphon off the water with a flexible tube or scoop it up using an improvised dipper. Alternatively, you can stuff a piece of cloth into the hole to absorb the water; and thereby, wring it from the cloth.

Water Supply Indicator (Plants)	Procurement Method
Moist Pulpy Centers	Cut off a section of the plant and squeeze or smash the pulp so that the moisture runs out. Catch the liquid in a container
Roots	Dig or pry the roots out of the ground, cut them into short pieces, and smash the pulp so that the moisture runs out. Catch the liquid in a container.
Vines	Cut a notch in the vine as high as you can reach, then cut the vine off close to the ground. Catch the dropping liquid in a container or in your mouth.
Fleshy, Stems, Stalks, and Leaves	Cut or notch the stalks, such as bamboo, at the base of a joint to drain out the liquid.
Air Plants	Within the American tropical forests, you may find large trees with branches supporting air plants. These air plants can hold considerable amounts of rainwater in their thickly growing overlapping leaves. Strain the water by using a cloth to remove insects and debris.
CAUTION: *Do not keep the sap from plants longer than 24 hours. It begins fermenting, becoming dangerous as a water source. As a rule, do not drink any liquid if it is sticky, milky, or bitter tasting. Purify the water before drinking it.*	

Image-45C: List of Water Sources in Plants

Sometimes, rock crevices and tree crotches gather and accumulate water. Apply the aforementioned procedures for obtaining the water. In dry domains, bird droppings around a crack in the rocks may indicate water in or near the crack.

Nevertheless, the most common water supply indicator is heavy dew. You can obtain it by tying around your ankles tufts of fine grass or rags, and then, walk along through dew-covered grass fields before sunrise. Wring the water into any clean container after the grass tufts or rags absorb the dew.

Still Structure & Set-up (Containment & Carriage)

A constant supply of water should be in place while you are in a survival mode. You do not want to quench your thirst or replenish lost body fluids inadequately. Besides, you can always drink whenever you feel, hydrating yourself if you have a ready water source or a system for containing water.

Solar water stills are effective and efficient water containment systems and carriers. In fact, you can set up your water still in any survival scenarios. You only need a minimum of certain materials to build one.

The working principle of the solar water still follows the basic concept of the *'greenhouse effect.'* It relies on the heat energy of the sun to pass through a transparent plastic barrier, which covers up vegetation and the ground.

The heat draws up moisture from the plant material and the ground through evaporation and rises to the underside of the plastic barrier, where it condenses and pours as water droplets. Since it is essentially collecting droplets, it apparently needs some time to let it accumulate water. Generally, it requires about 24 hours obtaining 0.5 to 1 liter of water.

You will have two options to build your solar water still. You construct either the aboveground solar water still or the underground solar water still type.

Aboveground Solar Water Still

Aboveground Solar Water Still Construction

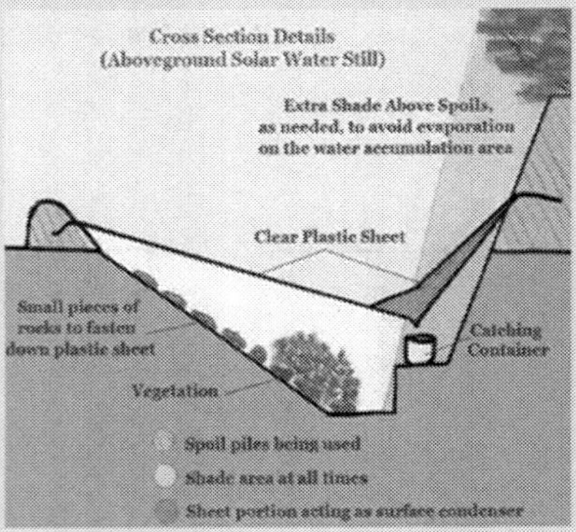

Materials/Resources:
- A sunny slope on which to situate the water still
- A clear plastic bag
- Green leafy vegetation
- Small pieces of rocks

Construction Procedure:
1. Fill the bag with air by turning the opening into the breeze.
2. Fill the plastic bag to about half to three-fourths full of green leafy vegetation. Ensure removing all sharp spines or hard sticks that might puncture the bag. Place the small pieces of rock or similar items to serve as weight to fasten down the bag onto the ground.
3. Close the bag and tie the mouth securely as close to the end of the bag as possible to keep the maximum amount of air space. If you have a piece of flexible tube or a small straw or a hollow reed, insert one end in the mouth of the bag before you tie it securely. Then tie off or plug the tubing so that air will not escape. This tubing will allow you to drain out condensed water without untying the bag.
4. Place the bag, with its mouth downhill, on a slope in full sunlight. Position the mouth of the bag slightly higher than the low point in the bag.
5. Settle the bag in place so that the rock works itself into the low point in the bag.
6. To get the condensed water from the still, loosen the tie around the bag's mouth and tip the bag so that the water collected around the rock will drain out. Then retie the mouth securely and reposition the still to allow further condensation. Change the vegetation in the bag after extracting most of the water from it. This will ensure maximum output of water.

Image-46: Aboveground Solar Water Still Construction

Underground Solar Water Still

Underground Solar Water Still Construction

Materials/Resources:
- A digging tool
- A clear plastic sheet
- Green leafy vegetation
- Cord or rope
- A straw or hollow reed
- Pieces of rock
- lumps of soil

Construction Procedure:

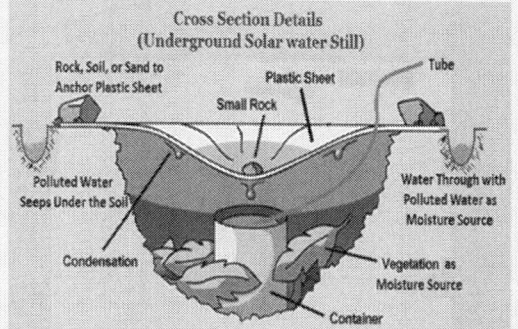

1. Select a soil site having high possibilities of containing moisture (i.e., dry streambed, a low spot where rainwater has collected). Such sites should be easy to dig. Ensure that sunlight must hit the site most of the day.

2. Dig a bowl-shaped hole about 3-feet (1-meter) across and 2-feet (60 cm.) deep. Dig further in the center of the hole to fit for the sump. The sump's depth and perimeter will depend on the size of the container that you have to place in it. The bottom of the sump should allow the container to stand upright.

3. Install the container upright in the sump. Anchor the tubing to the container's bottom by forming a loose overhand knot in the tubing. Extend the unanchored end of the tubing up, over, and beyond the lip of the hole.

4. Place the plastic sheet over the hole, covering its edges with soil to hold in place and to prevent the loss of moisture. Put a small rock in the center of the sheet. Lower the sheet into the hole until it is about 16-inches (40 cm.) below ground level, forming an inverted cone with the rock as its apex and directly over your container. Ensure the plastic cone does not touch the sides of the hole since the soil will absorb the condensed water.

5. Plug the tube when not in use so that the moisture will not evaporate. You can drink water without disturbing the still by using the tube as a straw.

NOTE: *If using plants as a moisture source, dig out from the sides of the hole to form a slope on which to place the plants. Then proceed as above. If using polluted water as the moisture source, dig a trough about 3-inches (8 cm.) wide × 10-inches (25 cm.) deep outside the hole and 10 inches (25 cm.) from the still's lip. Pour the polluted water in the trough. Do not to spill any polluted water around the rim where the plastic sheet touches the soil. The trough holds the polluted water and the soil filters it as the still draws it. The water then condenses on the plastic and drains into the container. This process works well when your only water source is salt water.*

Image-47: Aboveground Solar Water Still Construction

As cautionary measures, never use poisonous vegetation since it will likewise provide you with poisonous liquid. To satisfy your normal daily liquid requirements, you will need to build a minimum of three stills.

Sanitation Standards (Purification Processes)

Collecting rainwater in plants or in clean containers is generally safe for drinking. Nevertheless, you must purify water obtained from natural bodies of water like streams, springs, swamps, ponds, or lakes, and more importantly, water in the tropics or near human settlements.

By drinking non-potable water, you may or swallow organisms that can harm you or contract diseases. Examples of such diseases are dysentery, cholera, and typhoid. Common swallowed organisms are leeches and parasites borne from swallowed blood flukes.

As much as possible, purify all water you sourced from the ground or vegetation. There are many popular methods to purify water, but the most common is by applying chemical treatments of either chlorine or iodine, or by boiling. Boiling is the safest, most proven, and widely used water purification method. Another water purification method is herbal treatment, which can purify water from bacteria and viruses (refer to Image-48).

> ### Water Purification Processes
>
> **Heat Treatment or Boiling:**
>
> Bring water to a boil and allow it to continue boiling for 2 to 3 minutes. This allotted boiling time is enough to kill viruses and bacteria. However, boiling times can alter depending on your location. Boil water for 1 minute when you are at sea level. Add 1 minute for each additional 300 meters above sea level, or simply boil for 10 minutes regardless where you are.
>
> **Chemical Treatment:**
>
> Place 5 drops of 2% tincture of iodine in a 1-liter container filled with clear water. If the container is full of cloudy or cold water, place 10 drops. (Allow the container of water stand for 30 minutes before drinking.)
>
> **Herbal Treatment:**
>
> Peel some tomatoes and apples. Place the peelings in a rubbing alcohol solution for 2 hours. Let them dry out. As soon as they are thoroughly dried, place them into a container of water and let them sit for a few hours. Remove the peelings and enjoy.

Image-48: Most Common Water Purification Processes

Filtration Facility

Water filtration is the removal by suspending minute solid contaminants and/or bacteria from water through a mechanical process. The process describes letting water pass through a sieve or a filter bed, or the like.

However, these water filtration procedures only clear the water to certain degrees and make it more palatable. The bottom line is that you will still have to purify it.

If you found water to be stagnant, muddy, and foul smelling, you can filter and clear the water either of the following:

❖ By pouring it into a container and allowing it to stand for about 12 hours

❖ By pouring it through a water filtering system

To create a filtering system, you will be placing several layers of filtering materials such as charcoal, crushed rock, sand, and a piece of clean cloth in a hollow log or bamboo or a clothing material (refer to Image-49).

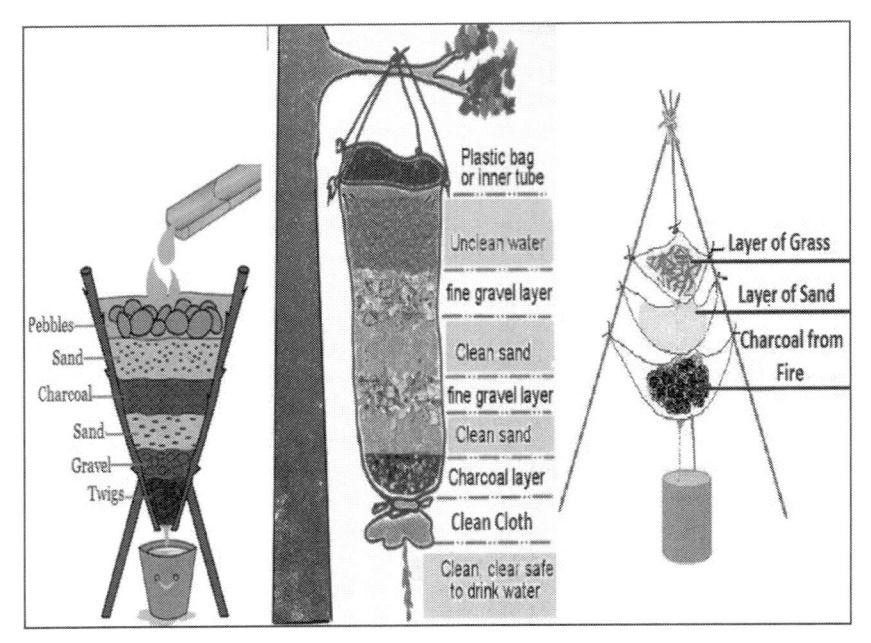

Image-49: Various Filtration System Devices

Removal of unpleasant odor from the water is through adding more solid charcoal pieces from your fire. Let it stand for 45 minutes prior to drinking it.

When in a radioactive environment, remember that you cannot remove radioactive contaminants from water through boiling or by any modes of disinfection. If you cannot obtain cleaner sources of water soon, you must filter some yourself.

Survival Skill # 3: Furnishing Food

In a survival scenario, it is highly advisable to be always on the lookout for the various familiar foods growing in the wild and live off the fats of the land and fresh produce of the sea. Trusting yourself of being able to go on surviving for days without food, as some sources would suggest, is ill-advised.

Essential to maintaining peace of mind and strength is to maintain your health through a nutritious and complete diet, even in the most severe and static survival scenario. Nature always has the food provisions you need that will allow you to survive any ordeal; that is if you do not eat the wrong plant or the wrong animal meat. Therefore, it would be to your advantage if you have a background of the plant and animal food provisions that are allowable and safe to eat.

Field Foraging

❖ **Plant Foods** – This type of food provides carbohydrates, which is the major source of energy of the human body. Among them are green leafy vegetables, roots or root crops, and other plant foods containing natural sugars (glucose) that provide your needed calories.

Several plants also provide sufficient proteins to maintain the body at its normal working efficiency. Prime examples of which are nuts and seeds.

While plants may not generally provide a balanced dietary regimen, they will sustain your nutritional requirements wherever you may forage for them, even in the Arctic region. One important plant you must not overlook is seaweed.

Seaweed is a typical formation of marine algae commonly found on or nearby ocean shores. Some freshwater varieties are also edible. It is a valuable source of vitamin C, iodine, and other minerals. However, an unaccustomed stomach consuming large quantities of seaweed can cause a severe laxative effect.

If you gather seaweeds for food, look for living plants floating freely or clinging to rocks. Seaweed washed ashore any period may be decayed or spoiled.

Preparing seaweed for consumption depends on its type. Dry tender and thin varieties in the sun; alternatively, you can place it over a fire until crisp. Crush the dried seaweeds and add them to broths or soups. You can also dry freshly obtained seaweeds for later use (food storing).

For thicker and leathery seaweeds, boil them for a short period until tender. You can consume some varieties raw after you have tested for edibility (refer to Image-33).

The food value of plants becomes more significant if you are in a survival scenario where wildlife is scarce. You can obtain plants more quietly and easily as opposed to animal meat.

❖ **Animal Food** – Meat is obviously more nourishing compared to plant food. Fact is that animal meat may even be more easily available in some survival scenario like the wilderness. In the seas, you can always have a galore of fish meat.

Nevertheless, to obtain animal meat, you should need to learn the habits of these meaty animals, as well as knowing how to capture various types of wildlife. To fulfill your immediate food needs, seek first the more easily obtained and abundant wildlife, such as reptiles fish, mollusks, crustaceans, and even insects.

These types of animal foods can readily satisfy your immediate hunger pangs while you prepare traps and snares for other larger game refer to Image-50A, 50B, 50C & 50D).

INSECTS AND WORMS

As the most abundant life form on earth, you can easily catch insects. Insects provide 65-80% protein compared to 20% for beef. As such, insects are an important, if not overly appetizing, food source.

Sources/Preparation:

Check stones, boards, rotting logs, or other materials lying on the ground. These sites provide a variety insects—ants, beetles, grubs, and termites— their excellent nesting sanctuaries.

Grassy areas, such as fields, are good areas to search because food insects like grasshoppers are abundant in these spots. Grasshoppers and beetles with hard outer shell have parasites. Remove any barbed legs or wings and cook them before eating.

You can eat most insects raw. The taste varies from one species to another. Wood grubs or beetle larvae, are also edible but bland. Some ant species store honey in their bodies, giving them a sweet taste. You can grind a collection of insects into a paste, mix them with edible vegetation, and cook them to improve their taste.

For worms, which are excellent protein sources, dig for them in damp humus soil or watch for them on the ground after a rain. Upon capture, drop them into clean, potable water for a few minutes. The worms will naturally purge or wash themselves out, after which, you can eat them raw.

NOTE: *Insects to avoid include all adults that bite or sting, hairy or brightly colored ones, caterpillars, and varieties having a pungent odor. Avoid also spiders and common disease carriers such as ticks, flies, and mosquitoes.*

Image-50A: Sourcing Insects & Worms for Food

CRUSTACEANS (Shrimp, Crayfish, Crab & Lobster)

Sources/Preparation:

Freshwater shrimp form large colonies in mud bottoms of ponds or lakes or mats of floating algae. Shrimp may come to a light at night where you can scoop them up with a net.

Crayfish are akin to crabs and marine lobsters. You can distinguish them by their five pairs of legs, the front pair having oversized pincers. Crayfish are active at night, but you can locate them in daytime by looking around and under stones in streams. You can also find them in the soft mud near the chimney-like breathing holes of their nests. You can catch crayfish by tying bits of offal or internal organs to a string. When the crayfish grabs the bait, pull it to shore before it has a chance to release the bait.

Lobsters and crabs are nocturnal and caught best at night. Find saltwater lobsters and crabs from the surf's edge out to water 40 feet (10 m) deep. You can catch lobsters and crabs with a baited hook or baited trap. Crabs will come to bait placed at the edge of the surf, where you can trap or net them.

MOLLUSKS (Barnacles, Bivalves, Clams, Chitons, Freshwater/Saltwater Shellfish, Limpets, Mussels, Octopuses, Periwinkles, Sea Urchins, and Snails)

Sources/Preparation:

You find bivalves similar to terrestrial and aquatic snails and freshwater mussel worldwide under all water conditions. River snails or freshwater periwinkles are plentiful in rivers, streams, and lakes of northern coniferous forests. These snails may be pencil point or globular in shape. Large snails, called chitons, adhere tightly to rocks above the surf line. Mussels form dense colonies in rock pools, on logs, or at the base of boulders.

In fresh water, look for mollusks in the shallows, especially in water with a sandy or muddy bottom. Look for the narrow trails they leave in the mud or for the dark elliptical slit of their open valves.

Near the sea, look in the tidal pools and the wet sand. Rocks along beaches or extending as reefs into deeper water often bear clinging shellfish. Snails and limpets cling to rocks and seaweed from the low water mark upward.

CAUTION: *Mussels can be poisonous in the tropics during the summer! Bake, boil, or steam them in the shell. They also make excellent stews in combination with tubers and greens. Never eat shellfish not covered by water at high tide!*

Image-50B: Sourcing Crustaceans & Mollusks for Food

FISH *(Freshwater & Saltwater Species)*

Fish provides a good source of healthy fats and protein. They are usually more abundant than mammal wildlife, and the ways to get them are silent.

Sources/Preparation:

You must know their habits to be successful at catching fish. They tend to feed heavily before a storm and not after, when the water is swollen and muddy. Light often attracts fish at night.

During a heavy current, fish will rest in places having an eddy, or near rocks. Fish will also gather under overhanging brush, in deep pools, and in and around logs, submerged foliage, or other objects that offer them sanctuary.

There are no poisonous freshwater fish. However, the catfish species has sharp protrusions on its barbel and dorsal fins that can inflict puncture wounds and quick infection. Cook all freshwater fish to kill parasites. Cook also saltwater fish caught within a reef or within the influence of a freshwater source as precaution.

Any marine life obtained farther out in the sea will not contain parasites because of the saltwater environment. You can eat these raw.

NOTE: *Certain saltwater species of fish have poisonous flesh. In some species, the poison occurs seasonally; in others, it is permanent. Examples of poisonous saltwater fish are the cowfish, jack, oil fish, porcupine fish, puffer, red snapper, thorn fish, and triggerfish. The barracuda, while not actually poisonous itself, may transmit ciguatera or fish poisoning if eaten raw.*

BIRDS

As with any wild animal, you must understand the common avian habits to have a realistic chance of capturing them. Knowing where and when the birds nest makes catching them easier.

Sources/Preparation:

You can take pigeons and other species by hand from their roost at night. During the nesting season, some species will not leave the nest even when approached.

Birds tend to have regular flying routes, going from their roost to a feeding area, to water, and so forth. Careful observation reveals where these flyways are and indicate good areas for catching birds in nets. Waterholes and roosting sites are some of the most promising areas for trapping or snaring.

All bird species are edible, but the flavor will vary considerably. You may skin fish-eating birds to improve their taste.

Image-50C: Sourcing Fish & Birds for Food

REPTILES

Reptiles are excellent protein sources. They are also relatively easy to catch. While you ought to cook them, you can eat them raw in a survival scenario. Their raw flesh may transmit parasites, but because reptiles are coldblooded, they do not carry the blood diseases of the warm-blooded animals.

The box turtle is a commonly encountered turtle that you should not eat. It feeds on poisonous mushrooms and may build up a highly toxic poison in its flesh. Cooking does not destroy this toxin. Avoid also the hawksbill turtle found in the Atlantic Ocean since its poisonous thorax gland. Poisonous snakes, alligators, crocodiles, and large sea turtles, however, present obvious hazards to you.

AMPHIBIANS *(Frogs & Salamanders)*

You can readily find frogs and salamanders around bodies of fresh water. Frogs seldom move from the safety of the water's edge. At the first sign of danger, they plunge into the water and bury themselves into the mud and debris.

There are only a few poisonous species of frogs. Avoid any brightly colored frog or one that has a distinct 'X' mark on its back.

Never confuse toads with frogs. You normally find toads in drier environments. Several species of toads secrete a poisonous substance through their skin as a defense against attack. Thus, never touch or eat toads to avoid poisoning.

Salamanders are nocturnal; so, the best time to catch them is at night using a light. Look for them in water around mud banks and rocks. They can range in size from a few centimeters to more than 2 feet (60 cm.) in length.

Image-50D: Sourcing Reptiles & Amphibians for Food

Preparation of Plant Food

Although some plants or plant parts are edible raw, you must cook others to be edible or palatable. Edible means that a plant or food will provide you with necessary nutrients; while palatable means it actually is pleasing to eat.

Many wild plants are edible, but barely palatable. It is a good idea to learn to identify, prepare, and eat wild foods. Methods used to improve the taste of plant food include soaking, boiling, cooking, or leaching.

Leaching is to crush the food (i.e., acorns), placing it in a strainer, and pouring boiling water through it or immersing it in running water. To remove the bitterness of acorns, leach them in water, if necessary.

Boil leaves, stems, and buds until tender, changing the water, if necessary, to remove any bitterness. Boil, bake, or roast tubers and roots.

When hard or dry, you may have to boil or grind them into meal or flour. The sap from several various trees, such as birches, walnuts, maples, and sycamores, contains sugar. You can boil these saps down to a syrup for sweetening. It takes about 35 liters of maple sap to make a liter of maple syrup!

Drying helps to remove caustic oxalates from some roots like those in the Arum family (i.e., taro, dasheen, cocoyam, tannia, and Mexican breadfruit). You can also dry fruits to preserve and augment stretching your food supplies.

Some nuts, such as chestnuts, are good raw; but they rather taste better when roasted. You can eat many grains and seeds raw until they mature.

Fishing Fundamentals

There are numerous methods to obtain fish in a survival scenario. You can create your own fish traps, fishhooks, and fishnets to help you catch fish.

Fishhooks

For creating fishhooks, you can improvise them from field-expedient fishhooks like small nails, wire, needles, pins, or any piece of metal. Alternatively, you can also use cut portions of tortoiseshell or seashell, flint, thorns, coconut shell, bone, or even wood as a fishhook material (refer to Image-51).

WOODEN FISHHOOK MAKING

1. Cut a piece of hardwood, roughly 6 millimeters in diameter and about an inch (2.5 cm.) long for forming the shank.
2. Cut a notch in one end, where you place the point (i.e., piece of bone, wire, or nail). Place the point in the notch.
3. Hold the point in the notch and tie securely so that it does not move out of position. This is a relatively a large hook.

For making smaller fishhooks, use smaller materials. A gorge is a small shaft of wood, bone, metal, or other material. It is sharp on both ends and notched in the middle where you tie cordage. Bait the gorge by placing a piece of bait on it lengthwise. When the fish swallows the bait, it also swallows the gorge.

Image-51: Procedure for Creating a Wooden Fishhook

Fishnet

You can improvise making a gill net if you have none available. Use a parachute suspension line or some similar material (refer to Image-52).

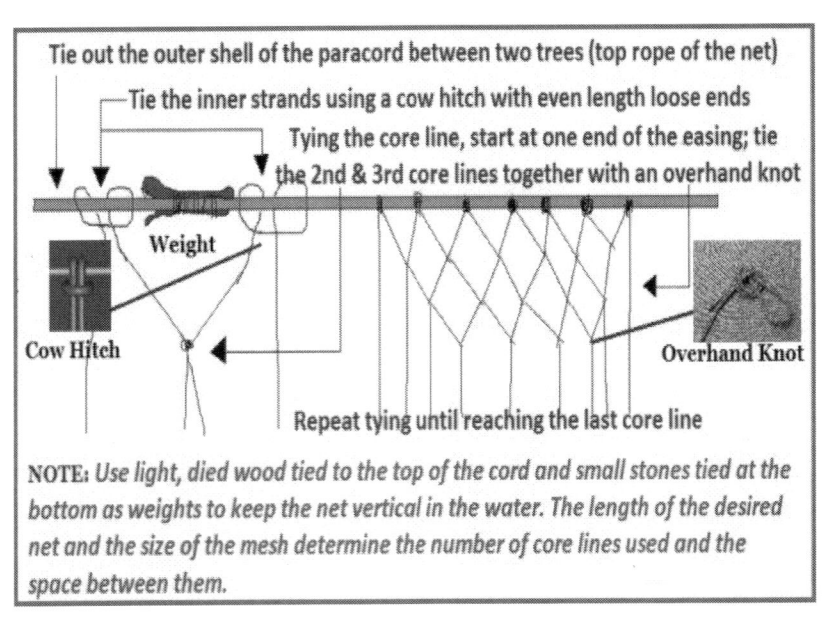

Tie out the outer shell of the paracord between two trees (top rope of the net)
Tie the inner strands using a cow hitch with even length loose ends
Tying the core line, start at one end of the easing; tie the 2nd & 3rd core lines together with an overhand knot

Weight

Cow Hitch

Overhand Knot

Repeat tying until reaching the last core line

NOTE: *Use light, died wood tied to the top of the cord and small stones tied at the bottom as weights to keep the net vertical in the water. The length of the desired net and the size of the mesh determine the number of core lines used and the space between them.*

Image-52: Procedure for Making an Improvised Gill Net

Fish Traps

You can trap fish by using several methods. The shore and tidal fish trap methods are both perfect for a large number of survivors in an area.

The concept of these methods is to block the openings when the tide recedes. On rocky shores, build natural rock pools. On coral islands, build natural pools on the surface of reefs.

On sandy shores, build ditches and use the sandbars to enclose. Build your trap as a low stone walling that extends outward into the water while forming an angle with the shore.

One method that is most common and easier to create is the basket fish trap. You can build it by lashing together several sticks with vines into a funnel-like shape. You will be closing the top end while leaving a hole at the other end, which is just large enough for a fish to swim through the trap (refer to Image-53).

Image-53: Basket or Funnel Fish Trap Description

During high tide, choose a good location where to fish. Install the basket fish trap at low tide.

Other Fishing Methods

SPEARFISHING

You can spear if you are near shallow water or about waist deep, where fish are large and plentiful. You can also fish in areas where the fish will gather or where there is a fish run.

To make a spear, cut a long, straight sapling. Sharpen the end to a point or attach a jagged piece of bone, knife, or any sharpened metal.

Alternatively, you can also make a spear by splitting the shaft a few inches down from the end, and then, inserting a piece of wood to act as a spreader. Sharpen the two separated halves to pointed ends.

Place the spear point into the water and slowly move it toward the fish. Thereafter, with a sudden push, impale the fish on the stream bottom. Never try lifting the fish with the spear, as it will most likely slip off and you will lose it. Hold the spear with one hand, and grab the fish with the other.

NOTE: *Do not throw the spear, especially if the point is a knife. You cannot afford to lose a knife in a survival scenario. Be alert to the issues caused by refracting light when looking at objects in the water.*

FISH POISON

Using poison for catching fish works quickly. It allows you to remain concealed while it is taking effect. It also enables you to catch several fish at one time.

When using fish poison, ensure to gather all of the affected fish since many dead fish floating downstream could arouse suspicion. Some plants that grow in warm regions of the world contain *rotenone*, a substance that kills or stuns cold-blooded animals but does not harm people who eat the targeted animals.

CHOP FISHING

During nighttime, when it has a good fish density, you can use a light to attract fish. Equipped with a machete or similar weapon, you can gather fish using the backside of the blade to strike them. Never use the sharp side since you will cut them in two pieces, and just end up losing some of the fish.

Hunting Handicrafts

Hunting larger game could be a problem at the sound of a rifle shot or for an unarmed survivor. As it is the case, trapping or snaring wild game is a perfect alternative. Several well-placed traps have higher potentials to catch more game than someone with a rifle will likely shoot.

For an effective performance of using any type of trap or snare, you should keep in mind the following:

❖ Be capable of improvising or setting up a proper trap

❖ Be familiar with the character and habits of the animal species you intend to hunt

❖ Not to alarm the prey by leaving traces or signs of your presence

You will have no catchall traps that you can set up for all animals. You must first determine the animal species in a given area before setting your traps intended for that specific animal. Look for apparently chewed or rubbed vegetation, droppings, feeding or watering areas, nesting or roosting sites, runs and trails, and animal tracks.

A simple snare composes a noose placed before an animal's den hole or over its trail and attached to a firmly planted stake. Use blades of grass or small twigs for holding your noose up if it is some kind of cordage placed upright along a game trail. Thick spider webs filaments are satisfactory materials for holding nooses open. Ensure the noose is large enough for an animal's head to pass over freely (refer to Image-55).

Image-55: Basic Animal Snare Description

While the animal keeps on moving, the noose tightens around its neck. The more it struggles, the tighter the noose gets. Usually, this basic snare does not kill the animal. If you use cordage, then it may slacken, enough to slip the animal's neck. Thus, the wire is the best option for your simple animal snare.

Supply Storage

You can retard food spoilage by drying plants through the wind or air, under the heat of the sun, or over a fire. Any of these methods will let you store or carry your plant food with you, and use them when needed. As for animal or fish meat, refer to Image-56.

> **Meat Preservation by Drying**
>
> Cut the animal meat into 6-millimeter strips with the grain. As an option, you can rub the strips with salt. Skew the meat strips or hang them on a rack in a sunny spot with unrestricted airflow.
>
> Keep the meat strips out of the reach of other animals or cover them to keep off blowflies. You can sprinkle chopped insect repellent herbs such as rosemary, basil, chives, chamomile, lavender, and spearmint.
>
> Allow the strips to dry thoroughly before eating. Adequately dried meats have dry and crisp textures. They do not feel cool to the touch.

Image-56: Preserving Meat thru the Drying Method

You can also extend the shelf life of foods in other ways such as freezing or by using the brine water or salt preservation methods. During cold climates, you can freeze and preserve meat for an indefinite period.

Freezing is not a way of preparing meat. You still ought to cook dried or preserved meat prior to eating it.

By using brine water or a salt solution, you can preserve meat by soaking it completely in a saltwater solution. The solution must thoroughly cover the meat. Optionally, you can use salt by itself; just wash the salt off the meat before cooking.

Survival Skill # 4: Forging Fire

In all survival scenarios, your ability to build a fire can make a great difference between dying and living. Fire can fulfill a thousand needs.

Foremost, fire can be a psychological booster since it provides companionship and peace of mind. It can also provide comfort and warmth.

Not only does it cook and preserve food but it also provides warmth by way of heating food, which saves calories that our body uses regularly to emit heat. Furthermore, fire is important for creating tools and weapons, sterilizing bandages, providing protection from animals, signaling for rescue, and purifying water.

Yet, fire can cause problems, as well. It can trigger forest fires or destroy all your belongings. When used inside shelters, it can lead to carbon monoxide poisoning or cause burns. Fire only implies that you should use it responsibly, and only when necessary.

Principles & Preparation

Creating a fire necessitates a survivor to have a better understanding of the basic principles of a fire. Fuel (in a non-gaseous state) does not actually burn directly. As you subject to heat a fuel, you produce gas. When this gas combines with oxygen in the air, it burns, and you create a fire.

The triangle concept of fire is essential in constructing and maintaining properly a fire. It represents the composite troika of the fundamental elements of fire—fuel, air, and heat. If you dispose of any of these, you will have no fire or the fire will go out.

The proper ratio of these components is very significant for a fire to burn to its optimal capability. The elemental ratio is not specific but rather, empirical. Therefore, practice is the only way to learn and come up with the balanced ratio.

Spot & Setup Selection

Building a fire in a survival scenario entails a number of considerations. First, you will have to decide what the right spot would be to build a fire. Second is the type of fire setup to use. Thus, you have to consider the survival area, its climate, terrain, and the tools and materials available. You will also anticipate how much time you have and why you need a fire.

In addition, when looking for the right spot to build a fire, inspect some important factors. Ensure it is a dry spot, protected from the wind, situated suitably to your shelter, and can focus the heat towards the direction you desire. Here are modes to set a fire on the various spots (refer to Image-57A, 57B, & 57C):

Underground Fireplace (Dakota Fire Hole)

In some instances, an underground fireplace will best suit your needs. It serves well for cooking food and conceals the fire.

1. Dig a fire pit in the ground.
2. On the upwind side of fire pit, dig an adjacent connecting pit for ventilation.
3. Build fire in the hole as shown.

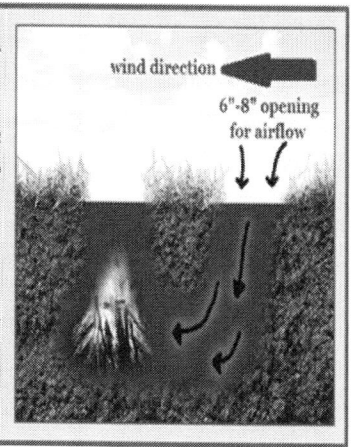

Image-57A: Building a Fire Underground

In Snow-Covered Areas

Use large, green logs to build a dry base for your fire. Trees with wrist-sized trunks become brittle and easily broken in extreme cold. Break or cut several green logs and lay them side by side on top of the snow. Add one or two more layers. Lay the top layer of logs opposite those below it.

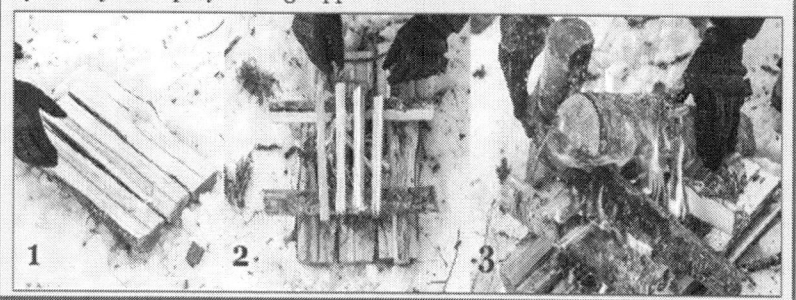

Image-57B: Building a Fire on Snowy Grounds

> **IN BRUSH-COVERED OR WOODED AREAS**
> Clear the brush and scrape the surface soil. Encircle the fire spot with rocks to form a fire ring or clear a circle at least 1 meter in diameter to prevent spreading the fire. As an option, and if time allows, construct a firewall by piling rocks or logs. The firewall also serves as a heat reflector, directing the heat where you want it. Besides, it will reduce flying sparks and the amount of wind blowing into the fire. However, you will need enough wind to keep the fire burning.
>
> Fire ring   Straight firewall   L-shaped firewall

Image-57C

Materials & Materialization

Besides having a good supply of wood or fuel in a survival scenario, you will need three types of fire materials for fire-building—tinder, kindling, and fuel. Tinder is a dry material such as straw and fine wood shavings or scrapings that ignites quickly with little heat. Essentially, a spark starts a fire.

Kindling, also called lightwood or fatwood, is a readily combustible material such as twigs, dry sticks or strips of wood to stoke a fire ignited by piles of tinder.

Kindling tends to increase the fire's temperature and at the same time, allows igniting slowly less combustible materials. Fuel is a less combustible material that burns gradually, yet steadily as soon as ignited. An almost essential material you must have in your survival supply is a charred cloth (refer to Image-58).

Charred Cloth Making Procedure

A charred cloth acts as fuel that holds a generated spark for longer periods. This allows you to put tinder on the hot surface to produce a small flame. Prepare this cloth in advance of any survival scenario. Add it to your personal survival kit.

You can make charred cloth by heating cotton cloth until it turns black, but does not burn. Once it is black, you must keep it in an airtight container to keep it dry.

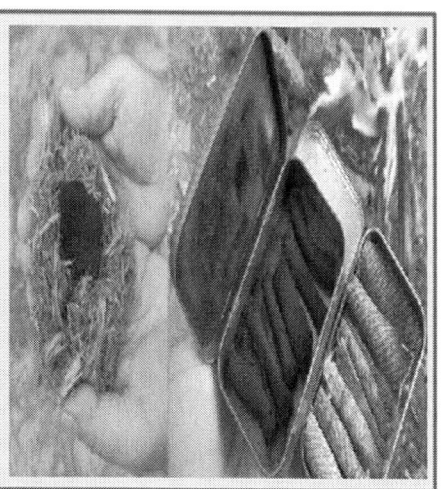

Image-58: Charred Cloth Making Description

You will have several options on how to build a fire and choose the type of laying a fire: tepee, cross-ditch, lean-to, and pyramid. Each of which has its own advantages.

However, the survival scenario you find yourself in will be the determining factor on which fire-laying type to use. To describe each type, refer to Image 59.

TEPEE

Arrange the tinder and a few sticks of kindling in the shape of a tepee or cone. Light the center. As the tepee burns, the outside logs will fall inward, feeding the fire. This type of fire burns well even with wet wood.

LEAN-TO

Find a log to serve as a lean-to member. Alternatively, you can push a green stick into the ground at a 30°-angle. Point the end of the stick in the direction of the wind. Place some tinder deep under this lean-to stick. Lean the pieces of kindling against the log or the lean-to stick. Light the tinder. As the kindling catches fire from the tinder, add more kindling.

PYRAMID

Lay two small logs or branches parallel on the ground. Place a solid layer of small logs across the parallel logs. Add three or four more layers of logs or branches, each layer smaller than and at a right angle to the layer below it. Make a starter fire on top of the pyramid. As the starter fire burns, it will ignite the logs below it. This gives you a fire that burns downward, requiring no attention during the night.

CROSS-DITCH

Scratch a cross about a foot (30 cm.) in size on the ground. Dig the cross about 3 inches (7.5 cm.) deep. In the middle of the cross, place a large wad of tinder. Build a kindling pyramid above the tinder. The shallow ditch allows air to sweep under the tinder, thus providing an air draft.

Image-59: Various Types of Fire Lay

Lighting a fire can also be technical. Always light your fire from the direction where the wind blows or from the upwind side. Ensure laying your tinder, kindling, and fuel, in order, for your fire to keep burning as long as you need it.

Igniters or devices that cause a spark provide the initial heat necessary to start the tinder aflame. These devices fall into two categories—primitive and modern methods (refer to Image-60& 60B).

CONVEX LENS
Apply this method only on bright, sunny days. The lens can be from a pair of eyeglasses, camera, binocular, telescopic sight, or magnifying glass. Angle the lens to focus the sun's rays on the tinder. Hold the lens steadily until the tinder begins to smolder. Blow gently the smoldering tinder into a flame.

METAL MATCH
Place a flat, dry leaf under your tinder with a portion exposed. Place the tip of the metal match on the dry leaf, holding the metal match in one hand and a scraper knife in the other. Scrape the knife against the metal match to produce sparks, hitting the tinder.

MATCHES & LIGHTERS
Ensure matches and lighters are waterproof. Store them also in a waterproof container along with a dependable striker pad.

BATTERY
A battery can generate a spark. This depends on the type of battery available. Attach a wire to each terminal. Touch the ends of the bare wires together next to the tinder so the sparks will ignite it. You can also use a strip of foil paper, if available, to attach both ends of any dry cell battery. It will burn out the middle of the foil paper, igniting the tinder.

Image-60A: Modern Ways of Igniting a Fire

FLINT AND STEEL

A direct spark method, it is the easiest and most reliable among the primitive ways of lighting a fire. Strike a flint or other hard, sharp-edged rock edge with a piece of carbon steel (stainless steel will not produce a good spark). This method requires practice and a loose-jointed wrist. As a spark has caught in the tinder, blow on it. The spark will spread and go into flames.

FIRE-PLOW

As a friction method of ignition, you rub a hardwood shaft against a softer wood base. To apply, cut a straight groove in the base and plow the blunt tip of the shaft up and down the groove. The plowing action of the shaft pushes out small wood fibers. Then, as you apply more pressure on each stroke, the friction ignites the wood particles.

BOW DRILL

Like all primitive fire-building methods, using a bow and drill is exhaustive since it requires you to exert much effort and be persistent to produce a fire.

Prepare first the fire lay before using the bow drill. Place a bundle of tinder under the V-shaped cut in the fireboard. Put one foot on the fireboard. Loop the bowstring over the drill or spindle. Place the drill in the pre-cut depression on the fireboard. Hold the bearing block on the top of the drill in position. Press down on the drill and saw the bow back and forth to twirl the drill.

Upon setting a fluid motion, apply more downward pressure and work the bow faster to grind hot black powder into the tinder, which catches a spark. Blow gently until it ignites.

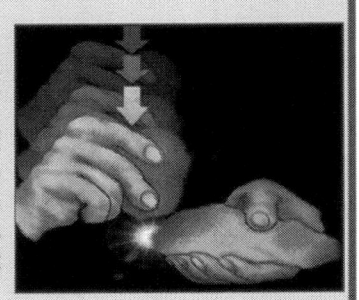

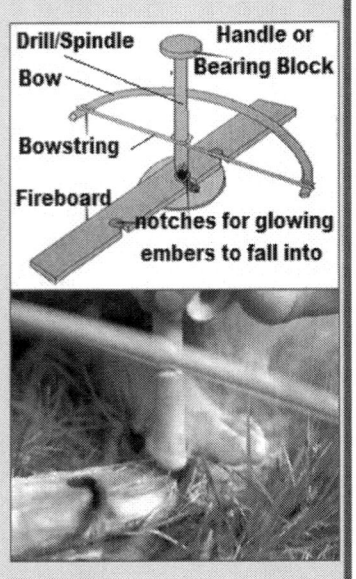

Image-60B: Primitive Ways of Igniting a Fire

Survival Skill # 5: Naturalist Norms

The more you understand and know about nature, the better chances you will have to survive in any survival scenario. To be successful at survival beyond the aforementioned basic survival skills also requires an in-depth naturalist knowledge of a variety of nature skills.

Apart from knowing to track animals and their instinctive characters so you can provide your food, natural healing using a variety of herbs and plants, locating available water sources, determining your direction using nature is as valuable as all the other naturalist norms previously discussed.

Natural Navigation & Determining Direction

In a survival scenario, you will be extremely lucky if you happen to have a compass and a map. If you do have these two pieces of equipment, you will most likely be able to move toward help.

What would happen then if you do not have all these? Much less, what would be the use of having both if you are not even proficient in using a compass and a map? You should learn the steps using the sun, moon, and stars to gain adequate navigational skills.

Several methods can determine your direction by only using the stars and the sun. However, these methods will only give you a general direction. You may come up with a more accurate direction if you have previous knowledge about the terrain of the area or country of the survival scenario.

Sun and Shadows

Fundamentally, the relationship of the Earth to the sun helps you to determine your direction. We have long been familiar that the sun ever rises in the east, as well as it ever sets in the west. However, there are a couple of seasonal variations.

At the northern hemisphere, the noonday sun—when the sun is directly at a perpendicular position relative to your spot and objects cast no appreciable shadows—will be due south. Shadows in this area rather move clockwise.

Conversely, in the southern hemisphere, the same noonday sun will be due north. Shadows move counterclockwise in this area.

Through a constant orientation practice, you can directly apply the shadows to figure out both time of day and direction. For determining direction, the shadow method presents two applications: the shadow-tip and watch methods (refer to Image-61A & 61B).

SHADOW-TIP OR STICK-TIP METHODS

The first application of the shadow-tip method is simple yet accurate. It requires you to find a 1-meter long straight stick and a level spot free of brush, where the stick will cast a definite shadow. Follow the steps to determine your direction:

Step 1: Put the stick into a level ground where it will cast a distinctive shadow. Using a rock or twig, mark the shadow's tip. This first mark is always west everywhere on Earth.

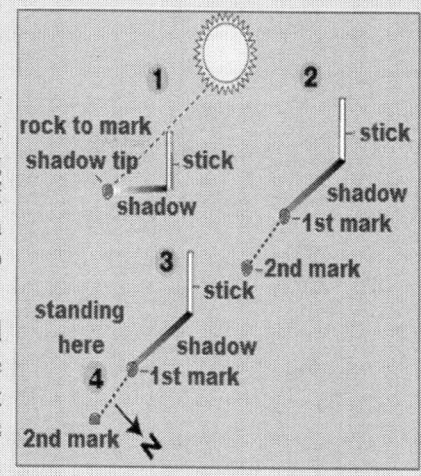

Step 2: Wait out for 10-15 minutes until the shadow tip moves a few centimeters. Mark the shadow tip's new position in the same way as the first.

Step 3: Draw a straight line through the two marks to obtain an approximate east-west line.

Step 4: Stand with the first mark (west) to your left and the second mark to your right. You are now facing **NORTH**. This fact is true everywhere on earth.

The second application of the shadow-tip method, also called as the *'equal shadow tip method,'* is more accurate but requires more time. Set up your shadow stick and mark the first shadow in the morning. Use a piece of string to draw a clean arc through this mark and around the stick. At midday, the shadow will shrink and disappear. In the afternoon, it will lengthen again and at the point where it touches the arc, make a second mark. Draw a line through the two marks to get an accurate **EAST-WEST LINE**.

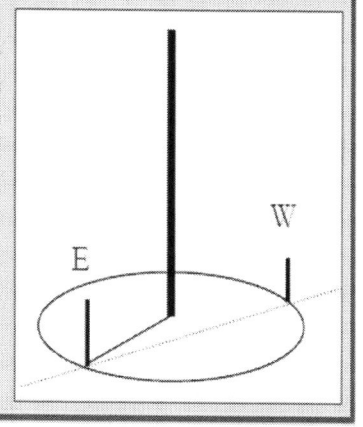

Image-61A: Orienteering Application Using the Stick-Tip Methods

THE ANALOG WATCH METHOD

Directions are accurate if you are using real local time without any changes for daylight savings time. Remember, the further you are from the equator, the more accurate this method will be. If you only have a digital watch, you can overcome this obstacle. Quickly draw a watch on a circle of paper with the correct time on it and use it to determine your direction at that time.

In the **northern hemisphere**, look at your watch to check the current time. Point your right arm at the sun. Pretend your arm is the hour hand of a watch. Now, point your left arm to the 12:00 position, based on the current time. Turn your body so that you are facing a direction that bisects the angle you just created. **NORTH** is behind you. You are facing **SOUTH**.

In the **southern hemisphere**, point your right arm at the sun. Pretend your arm is the minute hand of a watch pointing at 12:00. Now, point your left arm to the hour position that matches the current time. Turn your body so that you are facing a direction that bisects the angle you just created. You are facing **NORTH**.

NOTE: *If your watch is set to 'Daylight Savings Time,' subtract one hour.*

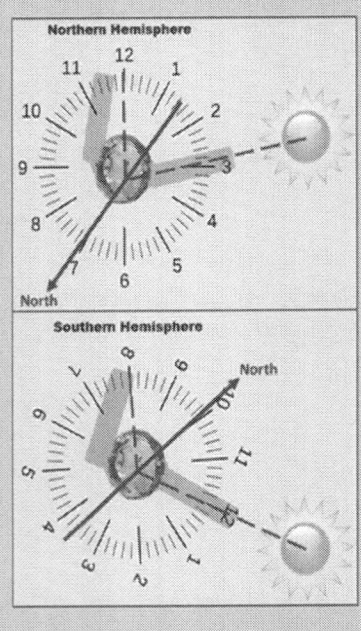

Image-61B: Orienteering Application Using the Stick-Tip Methods

Surveying the Stars

Your present location, whether you are within the southern or northern hemisphere, will determine which configuration of stars in the sky or the constellation you will use to identify the south or north direction (refer to Image-62A & 62B).

THE SOUTHERN SKY

Since there is no star that is bright enough to recognize easily near the southern celestial pole, you use the Southern Cross constellation as a reference to the south direction. The Southern Cross or Crux has five stars. Its four brightest stars form a cross that tilts to one side. The two stars that make up the longer axis of the cross are the pointer stars. To determine the general direction of south, imagine a distance five times the distance between these stars and the point where this imaginary line ends. Look down to the horizon from this imaginary point and select a landmark for you to navigate. In a static survival scenario, you can fix this location in daylight if you drive stakes in the ground at night to point the way.

Image-62A: Southern Sky Constellation

The Northern Sky

The Big Dipper, also known as Ursa Major or the Plow, and Cassiopeia are always visible on a clear night. Use them to locate the North Star, also known as Polaris or the polestar. The North Star forms part of the Little Dipper handle and can be confused with the Big Dipper. Prevent confusion by using both the Big Dipper and Cassiopeia together.

Cassiopeia is a 5-star constellation that forms the letter 'W' on its side. The North Star is straight out from Cassiopeia's center star. The Big Dipper and Cassiopeia are always directly opposite each other and rotate counterclockwise around the North Star in the center. The Big Dipper is a 7-star constellation in the shape of a dipper. The two stars forming its outer lip are the *'pointer stars'* as they point to the North Star.

Draw an imaginary line from the outer bottom star to the outer top star of the Big Dipper's bucket. Extend this line about 5 times the distance between the pointer stars. You will find the North Star along this line. After locating the North Star, locate the general north direction by drawing an imaginary line directly to Earth.

Image-62B: Northern Sky Constellation

Maneuvering thru the Moon

We can only actually see the moon when it reflects the brightness of the sun since the moon does not have a light of its own. When it orbits Earth along its 28-day circuit, we see varying shapes of the reflected light in accordance with its position.

We expect a presence of a new moon or an absence of it when the moon is at the opposite side of Earth from the sun. As the moon moves away from Earth's shadow, it starts reflecting the light of the sun from its right side and climaxes to become a full moon prior to waning or losing shape, appearing as a crescent on its left side.

Through this useful information, you can identify your direction. Whenever the moon rises before sunset, its illuminated side denotes the west. Whenever it rises after midnight, the bright side is the east. This lunar mechanics will provide you with an estimated reference of east and west during the night.

Distinctive Direction Determinants

The folkloric notion of determining the northern direction by the mosses growing on a tree is not accurate since moss can grow completely around the bark of trees. In reality, growth is lusher on the side of the tree that faces the north in the southern hemisphere and vice versa in the northern hemisphere.

For comparison, observe fallen trees around, and look at their stumps. On one hand, they manifest a more vigorous growth on the side facing towards the equator and their growth rings are more widely spaced. On the other hand, their tree growth rings are narrowly spaced on the side facing towards the poles.

Wind direction can also be helpful in some instances where there are prevailing directions and you know what they are. For example, a northerly wind will blow from north to south.

Identifying the variations between moisture patterns and vegetation on the south- and north-facing slopes can also help in determining direction. In the northern temperate zone, north-facing slopes are receiving lesser sunlight than south-facing slopes. In effect, they are damper and cooler.

During summer, north-facing slopes retain some patches of snow. In winter, trees and open areas on the south-facing slopes are first to melt their snow; thus, the ground snowpack is shallower.

"Patient endurance is the greatest life survival skills."

—**Lailah Gifty Akita**, Ghanaian activist, and founder of Smart Youth Volunteers Foundation

.

SIGNIFICANT SURVIVAL SCIENCES

"Extraordinary people survive under the most terrible circumstances and they become more extraordinary because of it."

—**Robertson Davies**, Canadian playwright, journalist, novelist, and critic

Being prepared in the event of a disaster or an emergency means being equipped with the adequate and proper supplies you may need. Keep all your supplies in an easy-to-carry emergency preparedness kit that you can use at home or take with you in case you must evacuate.

Nevertheless, there will also be situations when your supplies would be running out and some of your tools and instruments would be breaking or wearing out after certain periods in a survival scenario. In effect, you have to rely on some rudimentary lessons and ingenious techniques to back up your will to survive.

Aside from suggesting the most valuable items that you must prepare and include in your survival kit, this manual shares extra knowledge about two significant survival sciences that can tide you over to get the toughness in you going when the going gets rough. These useful fields of survival lessons are Bushcraft™ and Scoutcraft.

TOOLS OF THE TRADE (SURVIVAL SUPPLIES)

Your survival kit is an all-in-one package of basic survival supplies and tools that you prepare in advance to aid your survival in any emergencies. Once you have started stockpiling your survival gear, it can be difficult to determine what you are missing or unnecessarily doubling to your list.

Of course, each survivalist is much different, entailing different needs. Thus, no two survival kits or survival gear stockpiles are the same.

Never feel pressured into minimizing your list of survival gear or extending it by buying something that you do not really think you will be using. Instead, scan this manual's suggested list of items that you might have disregarded or skipped, or think would truly compliment your needs as a survivalist.

It is a systematic list of survival items recommended for safe travel. Besides, emphasizing portability and versatility, the list takes a functional approach in terms of a survivor's possible needs (refer to Image-63). Just the same, for your technical reference and most precious lifeline, never fail to **BRING WITH YOU THIS SURVIVAL MANUAL AT ALL TIMES!**

SUN PROTECTION:

100% UV protective sunglasses ("UV 400") | bandanna or scarf | lip balm | sunscreen for lips and skin (above 30 SPF)

INSULATION:

extra clothing for cold climates | gloves or mittens | hats (for snow and the tropics) | sweater or jacket

ILLUMINATION:

flare or unbreakable signal mirror (three fires in a triangle is the international distress signal) | headlamp or flashlight, batteries (use lithium cells only for superior shelf life) | high-powered LED light with replaceable batteries | laser pointer with lithium batteries | white lens with signaling capabilities

FIRST AID SUPPLIES:

First Aid kit | insect repellent

FIRE CRAFT:

butane lighter or matches or metal match | camp stove or portable gas burner and fuel such as bottled propane | charred cloth in a waterproof container

REPAIR KIT AND TOOLS:

bulletproof armor (used for protection in urban settings) | cable ties | candles | duct tape | heavy-duty needle and thread | ice axe for snowfield travel (if necessary) | knives | machete | multi-tool (Swiss Army knife) | plastic bags | pliers | scissors | screwdriver | hatchet | solar charger | sturdy cord or #550 parachute cord | trowel/shovel

EMERGENCY SHELTER:

bivouac sack | insulated sleeping pad | jumbo trash bags | lightweight poncho | plastic tube tent | space blanket | tarp

NUTRITION:

dried foods or canned goods | utensils for eating and cooking | snare wire

HYDRATION:

2-liters of water good for an extra day | portable water purification device | metal billycan or water bottles for water storage, boiling, purification, cooking

NAVIGATION SIGNALING DEVICES:

magnetic compass (or analog watch to determine orientation when the sun is visible) | mobile phone or two-way radio | optional altimeter or GPS receiver | pen/pencil and paper (for leaving notes to rescuers about the direction of travel) | surveyor's tape (orange-colored for marking the location for rescuers) | topographic map and trail maps/charts (if knowing the location in advance) secured in a waterproof container | whistle

Image-63: Comprehensive List of Survival Supplies

Flotation Facilities

If you happen to be in certain bodies of water and you do not have materials or the time to build a raft, you can use any of the various flotation devices to maneuver obstacles. Hereunder are items that you can use as a flotation device (refer to Image-64).

> **Cattails:** Gather stalks of cattails and tie them in a bundle, 10-inches (25 cm.) or more in diameter. The many air cells in each stalk cause a stalk to float until it will rot. Test the cattail bundle to ensure it supports your weight before using it.
>
> **Empty Containers:** Lash empty cans, water jugs, boxes, or other items together that will trap or hold air. Use them as water wings. Use this type of flotation device only in a slow-moving river or stream.
>
> **Logs:** Use a stranded drift log if one is available. Else, find a log near the water to use as a float. Be sure to test the log before starting to cross. Some tree logs, especially palm logs, will sink even when the wood is dead. Another method is to tie two logs about 2-feet (60 cm.) apart. Sit between the logs with your back against one and your legs over the other.
>
> **Ponchos and Plastic Bags:** Use your poncho and roll green vegetation tightly inside it so that you have a roll at least 8-inches (20 cm.) in diameter. Tie the ends of the roll securely. You can wear it around your waist or across one shoulder and under the opposite arm. You can also fill two or more plastic bags with air and secure them together at the opening.
>
> **Trousers:** Tie each trouser leg with a clove hitch at the bottom and close the fly. Using both hands, grasp the waistband at the sides and swing the trousers in the air to trap air in each leg. Quickly press the sides of the waistband together and hold it underwater so that the air will not escape. You will now have water wings to keep you afloat as you cross a body of water.
>
> **NOTE:** *Wet the trousers before inflating to trap the air better. You may have to re-inflate the trousers several times when crossing a large body of water.*

Image-64: Improvised Flotation Devices

You can devise several other flotation devices using your creative imagination. Just ensure testing the device prior to using it.

Bushcraft™ Basics

Bushcraft is all about surviving and thriving in the natural environment. This field of survival science also includes acquiring the knowledge and skills in doing so.

The basic Bushcraft skills involve hunting and tracking of animals, foraging for food, fishing, water sourcing, fire craft, shelter construction, and natural means of navigation, among others. The previous chapters have already discussed each of these topics. A couple of additional Bushcraft basics that are indispensable for your survival lessons are batoning and pioneering.

Batoning Branches

Learning to use tools with their proper applications is vital to survival. It is of no use carrying a certain tool if you do not know how to use it.

As a basic tool in survival, the knife has many applications. It can even replace a number of other equally significant tools with exclusive applications. For this reason, knowing how to execute batoning procedures by using only a knife is important. This saves you the burden of carrying other heavier and larger tools like a hatchet or machete.

Batoning is most useful for splitting wood for kindling, accessing a dry wood portion within a wet log, and producing desired forms of notches, boards, slats, or shingles. More importantly, it is a very helpful technique when chopping tools are unavailable.

The working concept of batoning, which is simply a woodcutting or wood splitting technique, is using a baton-sized stick, which you strike repeatedly on the spine of a sturdy knife to drive through the wood. In short, batoning is similar to the way you use a froe.

Pioneering Proficiencies (Cordage Craft & Lashing Lessons)

The art of using wooden spars and ropes joined by knots and lashings to create a functional structure is pioneering. Pioneering skills you should learn include lashing and knot tying.

Lashing

Lashing or cordage or rope work is a webbing or rope wire arrangement used to fasten and secure two or more items together in a rigid manner. Lashings most commonly apply to tie timber poles together, especially in Bushcraft or survival scenarios. The following are five major types of lashings that will be most helpful to you (refer to Image-65A, 65B & 65C).

Square Lashing has various sub-types used to bind spars together, usually in a crosswise position. However, all consist of a series of wraps around the spars; and then, fraps around the wraps between the spars.

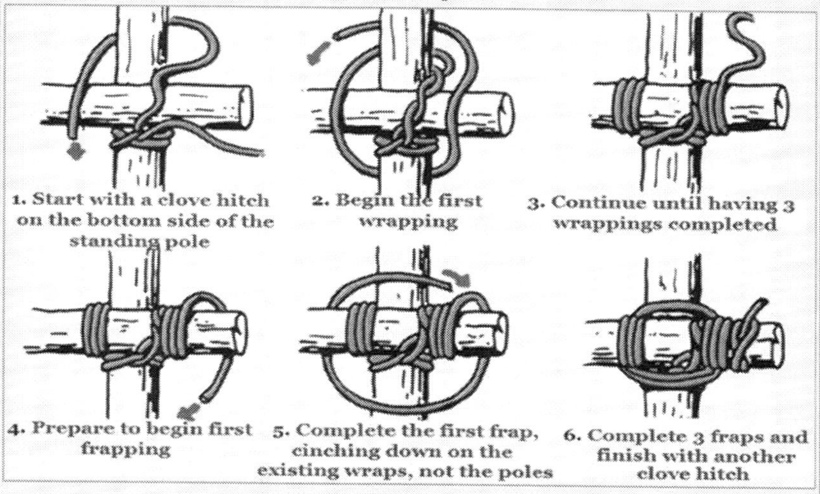

1. Start with a clove hitch on the bottom side of the standing pole
2. Begin the first wrapping
3. Continue until having 3 wrappings completed
4. Prepare to begin first frapping
5. Complete the first frap, cinching down on the existing wraps, not the poles
6. Complete 3 fraps and finish with another clove hitch

Diagonal Lashing is more useful for binding spars or poles together to prevent racking. Its turns of wrapping cross the poles diagonally and used to spring poles together where they do not touch.

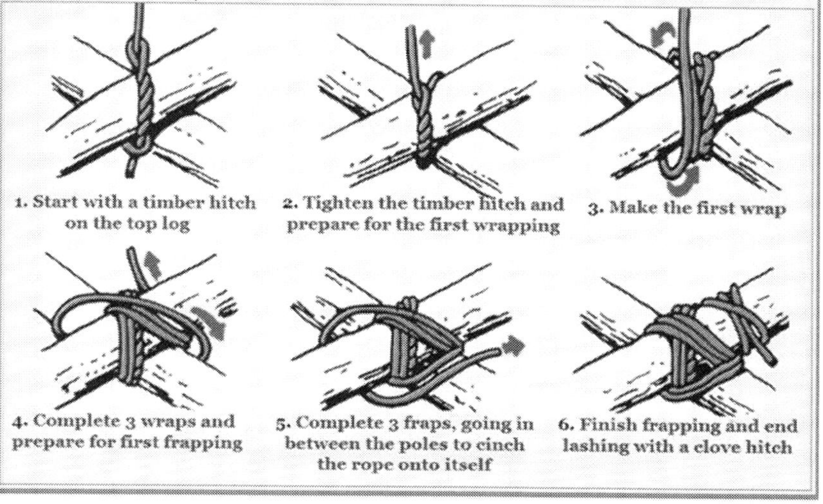

1. Start with a timber hitch on the top log
2. Tighten the timber hitch and prepare for the first wrapping
3. Make the first wrap
4. Complete 3 wraps and prepare for first frapping
5. Complete 3 fraps, going in between the poles to cinch the rope onto itself
6. Finish frapping and end lashing with a clove hitch

Image-65A: Square & Diagonal Lashing Descriptions

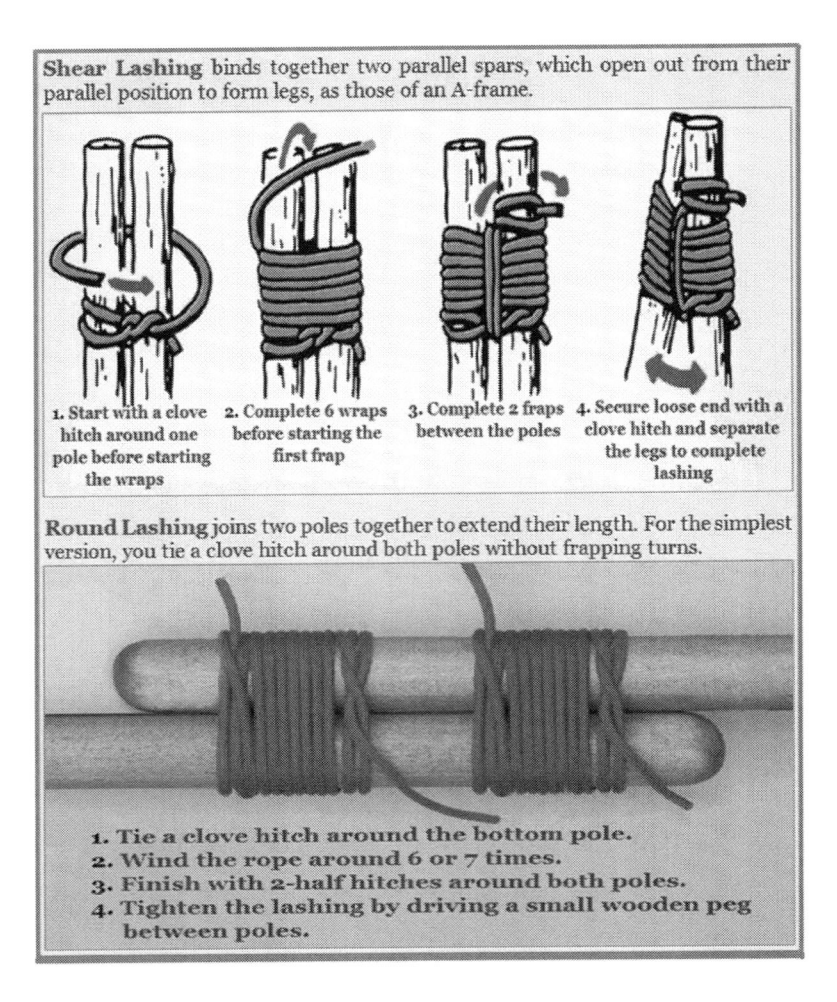

Shear Lashing binds together two parallel spars, which open out from their parallel position to form legs, as those of an A-frame.

1. Start with a clove hitch around one pole before starting the wraps
2. Complete 6 wraps before starting the first frap
3. Complete 2 fraps between the poles
4. Secure loose end with a clove hitch and separate the legs to complete lashing

Round Lashing joins two poles together to extend their length. For the simplest version, you tie a clove hitch around both poles without frapping turns.

1. Tie a clove hitch around the bottom pole.
2. Wind the rope around 6 or 7 times.
3. Finish with 2-half hitches around both poles.
4. Tighten the lashing by driving a small wooden peg between poles.

Image-65B: Shear & Round Lashing Descriptions

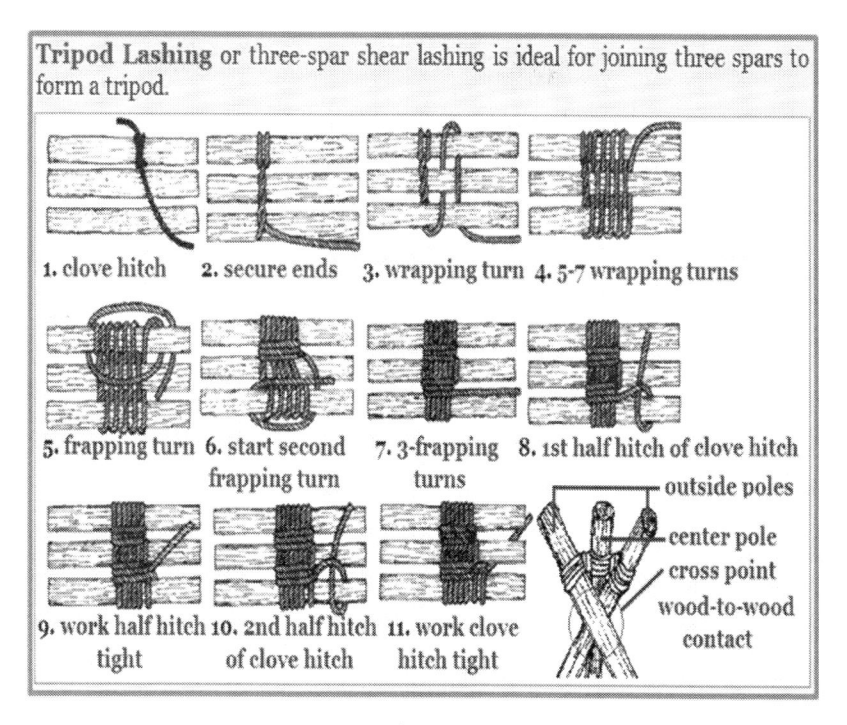

Tripod Lashing or three-spar shear lashing is ideal for joining three spars to form a tripod.

1. clove hitch
2. secure ends
3. wrapping turn
4. 5-7 wrapping turns
5. frapping turn
6. start second frapping turn
7. 3-frapping turns
8. 1st half hitch of clove hitch
   - outside poles
   - center pole
   - cross point
   - wood-to-wood contact
9. work half hitch tight
10. 2nd half hitch of clove hitch
11. work clove hitch tight

Image-65C: Tripod Lashing Description

Knot Tying

You may have heard that a rope is among the most valuable items of survival gear to include in your survival kit. However, you should know how to use a rope if you utilize it for survival. Otherwise, an improperly tied rope could lead to disaster.

Knot tying is simply tying rope. There are literally a thousand different ways to tie rope. Of course, you should not have to learn each of them. You only have to start mastering these five most useful survival knots (refer to Image 66A & 66B).

Square Knot (Reef Knot) is the easiest survival knot to tie. It also has the benefit of being flat when tied, thus, making it suitable for purposes where protruding knots would not work. However, it is not very secure; hence, never use this knot for tying two pieces of rope together or for load-bearing situations. Only use it for tying your rope around an object (i.e., tying bandages). Although it is not secure, its importance lays the foundation for tying all other important knots. To tie the square knot, just remember *'right over left, left over right.'*

NOTE: Both parts of rope must exit knot together

Clove Hitch is the most commonly used knot among the survival knots. Several other knots such as lashings derive tying procedures from a clove hitch. It is a type of jam knot meant for temporary uses. It will not be secure unless you have a load pulling on both sides. The greater the load, the more secure the clove hitch becomes. If you remove the load from one side, then the clove hitch will easily come undone. The beauty of the clove hitch is that it allows you to make it in advance before needing it such as securing quickly a rope to a post or tree.

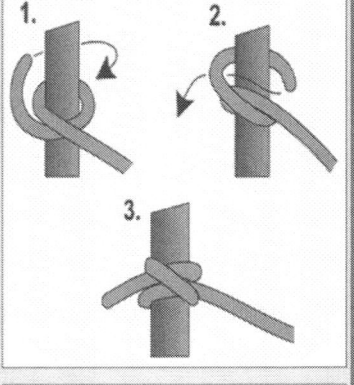

Bowline Knot is the *'King of Knots'* due to its importance. A type of loop knot, it forms a fixed *'eye'* at the end of a rope. Its virtues are both being easy to tie and untie. When subjecting a load, the knot becomes very secure. Although the bowline is generally a reliable knot, its main deficiencies are the tendencies to work loose when not under load, and to slip when pulled sideways. Its uses is for making a loop at the end of a rope, linking together two ends of a rope, fastening a line to a pole, attaching a rope to a tree for climbing, and securing a trap.

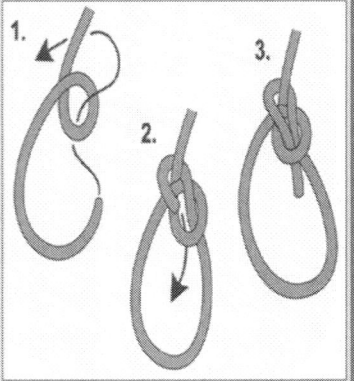

Image-66A: Square Knot, Clove Hitch & Bowline Knot Description

Carrick Bend is for tying two ends of the rope together. It works best when the ropes are of similar size such as when making nets and mats or joining the ends of two ropes together. It is very secure; but you must ensure that the ends of the two ropes are opposite of each other diagonally when tied. Else, the ropes could slip and the bend come undone! Once removing the load from the bend, the knot is easy to undo.

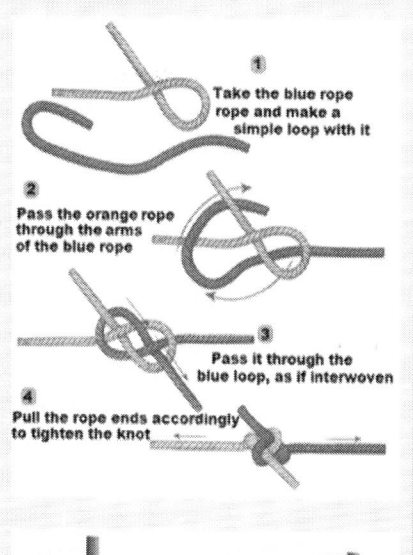

Distel Hitch is a type of friction or slide-and-grip knot. It slides around on a rope in one direction, but at the same time, grips securely when pulled in another direction. Climbers commonly use the distel hitch to attach a carabiner to a rope, allowing a climber to descend or ascend. However, it is also useful for moving safely large loads up or down a rope.

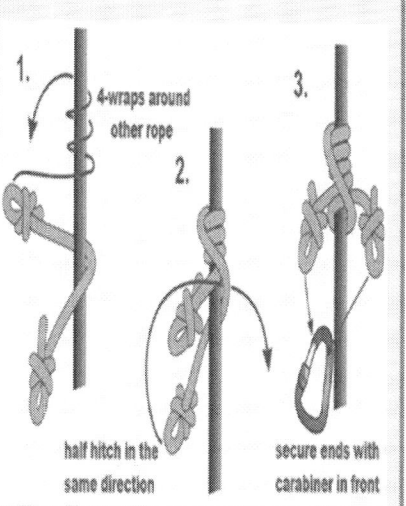

Image-66B: Carrick Bend & Distel Hitch Description

SCOUTCRAFT STAPLES

Scoutcraft covers a variety of skills and knowledge required by thrill-seeking individuals in venturing into wild country and sustaining themselves independently. Skills commonly associated with Scoutcraft are camping, first aid, cooking, wilderness survival, pioneering, signaling, and orienteering. The benefits of Scoutcraft are the following:

❖ Encourages self-reliance, resourcefulness, and confidence in your own ability

❖ Develops skills for application in the outdoors

❖ Provides training on what to do in emergencies

To complete your survival knowledge through Scoutcraft, you only have to enhance learning the last two skills— <u>making a compass</u> for orienteering outdoors and knowing how to perform visual signaling with the use of flags (<u>semaphore</u>).

Outdoor Orienteering (Compass Creation)

Your location within a survival scenario is your starting point towards your way back to safety and home. As discussed previously, nature can help you in this regard; but, what if nature acts crueler and denies you all these with cloudy skies?

You can construct an improvised compass as your last resort when you have a broken watch or when cloudy skies deny you the sun, moon, and stars (refer to Image-67).

Materials:
- a ferrous metal object (i.e., a flat double-edged razor blade or a sewing needle)
- a piece of non-metallic string (a piece of long hair will do) or something that floats (i.e., small wood or cork) from which to attach the metal object

OR
- an insulated electric wire
- a 2-volt battery

Procedure:
First, you have to polarize or magnetize the metal, say, a needle, by either manual or electromagnetic polarization.

Manual Polarization:
Stroke the needle slowly in one direction on a piece of silk. Alternatively, you can also stroke it carefully through your hair with deliberate strokes. Always rub it in a single direction only for about 20 minutes.

Electromagnetic Polarization:
Polarize electrically the needle using an insulated electric wire or a 2-volt battery. (If your wire has no insulation, wrap the metal in a thin strip of paper to prevent contact.) Form a coil with the electric wire and touch its ends to the battery's terminals. Repeatedly insert one end of the metal object in and out of the coil for about 10 minutes. Eventually, the needle will become an electromagnet.

Image-67: Creating an Improvised Compass

SOS Signaling / Semaphore

The primary purpose of signaling is to provide you with ways and means of communication in emergency-related situations, and navigational safety, particularly when language barriers arise. Among the most important signaling systems you should learn to use is the flag semaphore system.

Flag semaphore is a telegraphic communication system that conveys informative visual signals from a distance by the use of hand-held flags. For expedient situations, you can use rods, paddles, or even your bare hands. The position of the flags encodes the conveyed information, read when the flags are in a fixed position.

The modern flag semaphore system applies two short poles with square flags, which the survivor or signalman holds in various positions to signal numbers or letters of the alphabet. The survivor holds a pole in each hand and stretches each arm in one of the eight possible directions. When signaling, the flags should never overlap except when it is in the rest position—when the survivor stands upright with both poles in front, pointing down the ground. Flags are not actually required; their main purpose is simply to emphasize or make the signals or characters more obvious to the receiver (refer to Image-68).

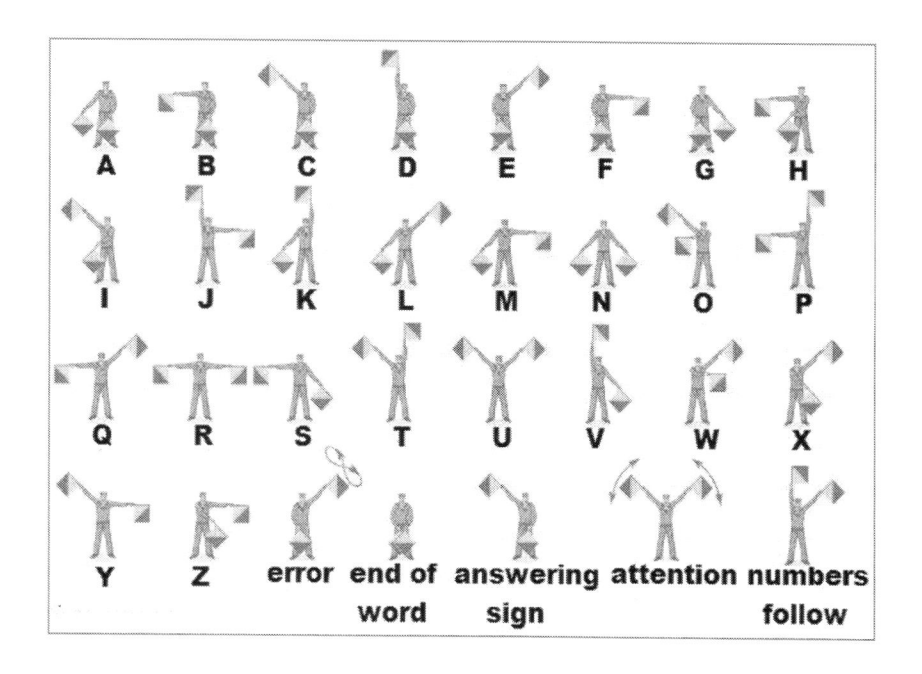

Signal numbers by first signaling *'numbers follow'* while letters by first signaling *'J.'* The signalman uses *'attention'* to request start a message transmission. In response, the receiver applies a *'ready to receive'*—raising vertically both flags overhead and then drops them to the rest position (*'end-of-word'*).

"People will do amazing things to ensure their survival."

—**Patricia Briggs**, American fantasy writer

Adaptive Capacity: A Conclusion

"It is not the strongest of the species or the most intelligent that survives. It is the one that is most adaptable to change."

—Excerpt from the *'Origin of Species'* by the Evolution Theory proponent, **Charles Darwin**

The art of survival begins neither by lighting a fire nor by building a shelter. Way before any of those skills, you should first prepare yourself by developing a solid mindset of a real survivor.

After all, survival is a battle; and, your tactical mission to triumph in any survival scenario is having the will to survive—to stay alive. As the great Chinese military strategist and general, Sun Tzu, once said, *'Know your enemy and yourself, and you can fight a hundred battles without disaster.'*

As you direct your attention to survival, you will be experiencing an assortment of emotions and thoughts. The faces and phases of anger, anxiety, depression, loneliness, fear, frustration, and guilt are all possible natural or impulsive responses to the several stresses common to survival. These reactions can either work for your success or work to your downfall.

When the survivor in you controls these reactions in a much healthier way, they will help you to increase your chances to survive. These positively altered responses prompt you to focus more on your survival lessons, to retaliate or defend when scared, to execute proper actions that ensure security and sustenance, to hope and keep faith with yourself and others, and to strive to survive and thrive against all odds!

When the survivor in you retains and sustains these reactions as they are, they will lead you to an impasse. Rather than rallying your internal resources, you will be listening to your internal fears. Right before the battle begins and long before you succumb physically, you already experience psychological defeat!

Take notice and review any real-life survival narratives. You will find out and learn that these survivors in each story shared similar psychological traits that allowed them to endure, if not, tolerate or adapt to their respective survival situations.

Actually, all of us are already equipped with the potent attributes that unite in shaping a survivor's mindset. We are not just aware that each of these attributes also presents a particular threat to their powers. Therefore, developing and nurturing a survivor's positive mindset is vital. In fact, your psychological attitude distinguishes the great difference between life and death.

In summary, the greatest and primordial survival skill is to **PREPARE YOURSELF!** You can never execute all the other basic survival skills and apply every textbook survival lesson if you have not prepared your mind, body, and spirit.

Not only it is important to learn to adapt and adopt the following virtuous attributes but also, learn the guile threats lurking behind each of them:

1. Positive Mental Attitude (PMA) is an utmost necessity. It is a critical priority for survival amidst the face of adversity; and therefore, it shall be your most significant skill to master.

Watch out though for *pessimism* to creep in. It can overwhelm you and in deviating your focus towards the unpleasant and negative sides of a situation. Deal with it and stay positive as much as you can while you maintain a strong grip on reality.

2. Mental Toughness is your strong will and resolute mind. Survival is not all about your physical prowess, but rather, you have to be tough mentally. Suffer the insufferable and tolerate the intolerable! Overpower your weakness and your desires of giving up!

Watch out though for a *declining psychological capacity*. Always do whatever you can in the best way possible to avoid yielding in and shutting down.

3. Motivation is what motivates you to stay alive whenever everything goes wrong. Seek your own motivation. It may be your faith, family, or friends. Hope for the best and expect the worst. After all, everything in life is a play and comes unrehearsed.

Watch out though for *hopelessness*, which is motivation's poison. You will be lost in oblivion if you lose hope that your God has completely abandoned you or you never believe to be back in safety and reunited with your loved ones.

4. Working Ethics and Principles are principal aspects of a survivor's mentality. Similar to learning other skills, you can develop your work ethics over time, even if you are lazy. Undergoing a difficult experience or situation can teach you to work better and harder the next time around; that is if a next time comes along.

As a survivor, you should have an effective work ethic of sticking out working on the job or a bad situation until done. This can go a long, long way in resolving matters that luck never provides.

Watch out though for *indolence*, which is not disposed to exertion, activity or work, but rather, seeking always for the easiest way out. Never be lazy lest going into trouble that will be more serious. Make use of your time and make the best out of everything.

5. Adaptability and survival are always inseparable. Reflect on the survival of living organisms. Those that could not adapt to an ever-changing and evolving environment have ultimately expired. Those that could readily change and evolve have always survived.

You have to live with the situation and make it your safe home before you can leave the situation and make your way back safe home.

Adapt to changing events, environments, and situations. Recognize those things worth continuing and those needing abandonment.

Watch out though for taking *stubbornness* into action. Sometimes, stubbornness can be either positive or negative. It can be a persistence to live or a refusal to adapt. Be the former and have the stubbornness to die.

You only have to bear in mind that you must never be afraid to change… instead, alter your mind to alter the way you live, for the better, forever.

Believe that life is long you will never squander these attributes, as well as your time. Most of the time, you are actually not living life, but simply, existing… only allowing life to happen to you rather than taking the reins to live the life you so want and deserve to live.

Life is long if you only know how to use it. Learning how to live life takes a whole life. In the same way, it might surprise you more knowing that it takes a whole life to learn how to die.

"We shall draw from the heart of suffering itself the means of inspiration and survival."

—**Sir Winston Churchill,** British Prime Minister

Printed in Great Britain
by Amazon